D0058382

WITHDRAWN

# On
# TIME

# On TIME

## A PRINCELY LIFE IN FUNK

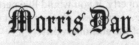

Morris Day

WITH

DAVID RITZ

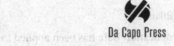

Da Capo Press

Copyright © 2019 by Morris Day
Frontispiece photograph courtesy of Allen Beaulieu, © 1981 A. Beaulieu
Jacket design by Alex Camlin
Jacket photograph by Deborah Feingold
Jacket copyright © 2019 by Hachette Book Group, Inc.

Hachette Book Group supports the right to free expression and the value of copyright. The purpose of copyright is to encourage writers and artists to produce the creative works that enrich our culture.

The scanning, uploading, and distribution of this book without permission is a theft of the author's intellectual property. If you would like permission to use material from the book (other than for review purposes), please contact permissions@hbgusa.com. Thank you for your support of the author's rights.

Da Capo Press
Hachette Book Group
1290 Avenue of the Americas
New York, NY 10104
HachetteBooks.com
Twitter.com/HachetteBooks
Instagram.com/HachetteBooks

First Edition: October 2019

Published by Da Capo Press, an imprint of Perseus Books, LLC, a subsidiary of Hachette Book Group, Inc. The Da Capo Press name and logo is a trademark of the Hachette Book Group.

The publisher is not responsible for websites (or their content) that are not owned by the publisher.

Print book interior design by Jeff Williams.

Library of Congress Cataloging-in-Publication Data has been applied for.

ISBNs: 978-0-306-92221-3 (hardcover), 978-0-306-92220-6 (ebook)

# CONTENTS

# On TIME

# PRELUDE

PRINCE is the first word in this book. I place him first because he's my biggest influence, the person who most powerfully shaped my musical life. He's also first because of our brotherhood. Our bond was something else. It began strong and got even stronger. Then strong changed to strange and strange turned to strained. Yet the bond never broke.

I'm also putting Prince first because, though he's gone, he's still here. I still hear his voice in my head. I can't write this book without his voice. And rather than keep that voice to myself, I'm going to share it with you. I have no choice. Anything else would be cheating Prince. He wants to be heard.

I'm no mystic. I'm not saying that I have the power of telepathy or can communicate with souls on the other side. I don't and I can't. But I swear on my sacred pearl-white DW drum set that every time I sit down to start telling my story, I hear this motherfucker whispering in my ear. He won't leave me alone. Won't be quiet. Won't be left out of this trip. So I'm taking him along. I'm letting him in. Gonna let you hear the voice that I'm hearing.

I'm hearing him say, *Good decision, bro. & I'll tell u y. More folks r more interested in reading 'bout me than u.*

Agreed.

*Then what r u gonna do about it?*

Write about you, bro.

*That means u'll b putting words in my mouth.*

You'll give me those words.

*But that means u get 2 make up & twist my words.*

Promise I'll be true to you.

*Still nervous about this whole situation. I don't like how* u *can write this thing up any way u wanna. U got a power I no longer have.*

You ain't lost none of your power. I feel you. I know you.

*Wrong. No one really knows me.*

Shit, I know your silly ass as well as anyone. We been knowing each other since we were kids. I feel like you're part of me.

*There r people who say I made u.*

Those "people" are you. You're the one saying that you made me.

*Well, didn't I?*

Well, maybe. And maybe not. But sure, to a large extent.

*2 such an extent that u'd have no story without me. Truth is, u can't tell your story without me.*

So you see my point.

*U just being slick.*

Being truthful.

*But your truth & my truth r hardly the same.*

You gonna have your say. I'll let you say whatever you want.

*Not worried about what I say. Worried about what u gonna say.*

I'm gonna give you your props—and not just 'cause I got your spirit breathing down my neck as I write this book. Gonna give you your props 'cause you deserve them. You done changed up the game. You sculpted a sound. You formed a musical universe. I'm lucky to have slipped into that universe.

*I believe I've been in your ear ever since u chased me down 2 get in my band.*

Hell, man, you asked me in.

*U hustled your way in.*

I had the chops to kick your drummer's ass. That's how I got in.

*Point is, bro, I let u in. Ain't no disputing that.*

Who's disputing? These days before my show starts, I put your pretty face up on the big screen. Then I tell the crowd how we miss you, how we love you, how you're the Founding Father.

*But what else u gonna say about me in this book?*

That we brothers. Always have been. Always will be. I'm the one cat who wasn't scared to tell you what I thought. And in this book, that won't change. Gonna be true to you but also true to me. And if I'm not mistaken, I do believe that's why you kept me around. I said what was on my mind, whether you liked it or not. Remember when you played "When Doves Cry"?

*Yes indeed. U said, "Don't play me nothing else unless it's funky. & if u do put out that Dove song, put some bass on it."*

Right. Wasn't trying to kiss your ass. Others might have done that, but not me.

*U didn't kiss my ass, but when it came 2 "Dove," u had your head up your ass. Was my first #1 pop single.*

I don't give a shit. Still think it needs some bass.

*So we gonna keep arguin', is that it?*

We gonna do what we gonna do.

*Which is just what led 2 all the fights & the fallings-out. Is that something u really wanna get into?*

Why not? Brothers love each other, but brothers fight. Brothers fall out.

*But our fights & fallings-out left deep wounds.*

Wounds that need to heal.

*Or not b reopened.*

They were already open when you turned me into your arch-enemy in your movie. You made me your foil.

Purple Rain *made u famous.*

Hell, yes. *Purple Rain* made me $50,000. How many millions did it make you, bro?

*U made out fine. So fine, in fact, that u get 2 do a book. Only problem is that u using me 2 get more people 2 read your story.*

Yet if I told this story without you, you'd be pissed.

*Any way u look at it, I'm not about 2 let u flip the script 2 suit your purpose.*

Settle down, man. Just wanna tell it right.

*Well, if that's your true aim, u'll need me 2 check u along the way.*

Exactly. So now that we're on the same page, let's turn the page.

# 1

# DROP THE GROOVE

The groove is the main thing 'cause the groove is what keeps us going.

The groove has always kept me going. I speak as a drummer when I say that groove is born out of the One.

The One's the moment of maximum impact. The kick. The hook. The anchor. For me, those first Jackson 5 records were all on the One. James Brown was on the One. James Brown's drummers Jabo Starks and Clyde Stubblefield were on the One. Tower of Power's drummer David Garibaldi was no doubt on the One. With their magic sticks, these drummers cracked my head open.

The One came early in my life and stayed. The groove hit me hard. The groove sustained me. Still does.

*I never doubted your chops as a drummer. Even said so in an interview with* Rolling Stone. *Said Morris Day has big chops on drums.*

But then right after you got your record deal and formed a band, you chose a drummer you knew I could outplay.

*Wasn't just a matter of who played better. That band needed a certain look. I got 2 your look later. I recognized your talent. U can go on & brag about it.*

Not bragging, just saying I found my groove early on.

As a kid, it wasn't school or books or church that got to me. It was the groove. From Jump Street, I was dancing in front of the TV in my Fruit of the Looms the second James Brown came on *American Bandstand.* Man, I'd be banging out beats on my mama's couch, beating on her pots and pans, chasing down the rhythms, playing with syncopations the way other kids play with toys. Hit the beat so hard I made a big hole on the arm of the couch. Mom said, "Either I gotta get that little boy a drum or I'll kill him." So Mom, bless her heart, got me a toy drum set. Got it when I was four. My cousin busted it up but I kept on keepin' on. Kept bangin' with spoons, forks, and knives. Ridin' those rhythms. And using those rhythms to hide from a confusing childhood.

Was born December 13, 1956, in Springfield, Illinois. My mother, Lavonne Daugherty, married Richard Sylvester Day—called Dickie—when she was sixteen. My sister, Sandy, eighteen months older than me, was their other child. By the time I came along, though, my parents had divorced. My father had returned from the air force, where he was stationed in Germany, and hooked up with a woman named Shirley. He gave me two half-brothers and a half-sister and was living in Decatur, some forty miles away. Saw him on a couple of short summer vacations, but that was it. Can't say I'm bitter. Can't really say how I feel. The man just wasn't around. Left a void. Left Mom to fend for herself in the projects.

*R u really going thru all your family history? People wanna get 2 the part where u meet me. Don't bog us down with details.*

Get outta my face and let me set this thing up right.

When you first heard the story, I remember you listening hard. You related. Your daddy issues were different than mine, but you had 'em. You had 'em big time.

My big daddy issue wasn't as much my biological father as the dude Mom married next. They had a son—Jesse Jr., my little brother and lifelong best friend—in 1960. Jesse Hamner Sr. was a scary cat. By then Mom had her GED and had gone to school to become a registered nurse. She had a good gig but a bad husband. He was a drinker, gambler, and abuser. The cops were always showing up to break up their fights. Sandy, a fighter herself, once smashed a heavy glass ashtray on Hamner's head. I was too little to do anything except soak up the terror. Seeing some dude beat up your mom is nothing you'll ever forget. He also had no patience with me. When Mom worked the late shift and left us alone with him, I'd start crying. I'd cling to my mother and beg her not to go. Hamner hated that. He called me a punk, and after she was out the door, he'd slap my face. He was a scary menace. Made my life miserable.

At the same time, Mom loved her kids. She doted on me. She used to talk about how my granddaddy was a pimp, and maybe with him in mind, she dressed me accordingly. My Sunday-go-to-meeting church outfits were slick: two-toned shoes, pinstriped suit, snappy little hat, long chain hanging out the pocket. Looking sharp came early and came natural.

Mom was a young woman who liked living a big life. She and Hamner loved hosting parties at the crib. I have happy memories of hearing the Isley Brothers playing on the box and smiling folks drinking and dancing up a storm. But sad always overwhelmed happy. Hamner's violence got worse. Shit got so bad that Mom arranged to secretly ferry all of us out of Springfield. Happened in 1964 when I was seven. Mom decided that despite her excellent position as an RN at St. John's Hospital, Hamner had gotten too dangerous. Time to get outta Dodge.

We left town on the down-low, Mom scrambling to get us ready to split before Hamner could find out and do something crazy. Middle of the night, car trunk filled with whatever we could stuff in there, Mom, Sandy, me, and baby bro Jesse riding across the dark country—radio blasting Mary Wells braggin' 'bout "My Guy," Little Anthony and the Imperials singin' 'bout "I'm Going Out of My Head," Ray Charles cryin' 'bout being "Busted"—all the way up to Minneapolis. Start of a whole new life.

# 2

# CROWDED HOUSE

*How long u intend 2 go on with this childhood thing?*

When you gonna calm your nervous ass down? Just chill.

*Get 2 the hook.*

It's not like writing a song. Besides, you ain't writing this book.

*There's no book without me.*

You said that shit before.

*Ignore me at your risk. Ignore me & u'll lose your readers.*

Not ignoring anyone, especially you. Not that many years pass in Minneapolis before I meet you. Well, actually, I heard you before I met you.

*& what'd u hear?*

A crazy talented guitarist.

*Talk about it.*

I'll talk about it in a minute.

*Talk about it now.*

You a controllin' fool.

*I'm a hitmaker. U wanna make this book a hit? Well, hit 'em with a guitar lick.*

Your licks were like lightnin'. Thunderbolts. Jimi Hendrix licks. Jimmy Page licks. Carlos Santana licks. Screamin' licks that made me think you had to be older than you were. Old blues licks but refashioned to sound new and fresh. High-drama licks. Panty-dropping licks. Licks the chicks went crazy for.

*& licks that made u wanna b in my band.*

No doubt. But give me a lil' room to breathe, homeboy. I'll get to your music. But meanwhile, there's shit I still need to explain. I haven't even gotten to Minneapolis yet.

I never thought Minneapolis was gonna be our permanent home. When we left outta Illinois, I had California in mind. Mom always talked about it as the Promised Land. I needed no convincing. I saw it as sunshine, swimming pools, and movie stars. LA was *77 Sunset Strip*, where Elvis had a big house in the hills and where the surf was up and the living easy.

"We'll get there," Mom said. "Minneapolis is just a stopover."

But it wasn't. Minneapolis proved as permanent as a block of concrete. We were there to stay. Because there was reciprocity between RNs in Illinois and Minnesota, Mom got gigged up in a hurry.

When we first arrived, Aunt Regina, Mom's cousin, took us in. Strangely, she and Mom had married brothers. Regina's husband, Spike, was the sibling of my dad, Dickie Day.

Regina and Spike had six kids. We rented the top floor of their house. So there we were, nine kids running around supervised by a few adults. The adults were doing some running around of their own.

Turned out Uncle Spike worked at a gas station owned by Joe Buchalton, a hustlin' brotha whose other properties included a supermarket in the hood, a car-detailing shop in St. Paul, and a small office complex plus a partnership in a prostitution operation—not to mention moving drugs while handily hijacking trucks. Joe was busy. So was Uncle Spike, who wound up with Joe's wife. That was okay with Joe, though, because he hooked up with my mother. Betrayal and spouse-switching is confusing enough for adults, but imagine what it did to ten-year-old me. Killed my trust in women. Killed my trust in men. Had me scrambling for sanity in an insane situation.

Spike, my father's brother, was now bedding my future father's wife while my future father was bedding my mother. Keep in mind—a lot of this switching was happening in secret before it came out in the open. That only added to my mind fuck. When it was all sorted out, we were living in Southside Minneapolis before eventually moving to the Northside, me working at Joe's gas station and wondering whether everyone's family was as crazy as mine.

Mom was a spark plug, a smart young woman looking to live life to the fullest. Looking back, I can't blame her for anything. And I don't. She was ambitious, and in a few years, her ambition would serve me.

*Now r u gonna talk about her trying 2 manage my band?*

Ain't there yet.

*Well, hurry.*

While Mom was moving around, trying to figure out how best to manage her children and deal with her new husband, Joe, sister Sandy did a lot of the mothering. She looked after me and Jesse. It was Sandy who got me into a choir.

*& started writing love lyrics 4 some of my songs.*

You're still rushing. That comes later. Before we even heard of anyone called Prince, Sandy had joined the Nation Time Choir. This was the end of the '60s, when radical politics was sweeping through the hood. Before they started singing, Nation Time members listened to Malcolm X sermons. They went to prisons to sing for inmates incarcerated on bullshit charges. They were out to do good. They were also caught up in the black-is-beautiful dashiki-wearing Afrocentric fever of the times. Joining the choir meant changing your name. Sandy was Akua Binta and I became Kashke Nagomo. Beyond music, we were all taught martial arts. There was a strong Black Panther vibe. Backing the choir was a band called Midwest Express with a badass drummer.

I went along with Sandy—singing with thirty other brothas and sistas was fun—but my eye was always on the drummer. That's what I wanted to do. Malcolm X was an intellectual firebrand and I could appreciate his rage. But my heart was with Sly and the Family Stone talkin' 'bout "Hot Fun in the Summertime." I popped outta the choir a few months after joining. Politics wasn't my thing.

The beat kept turning me toward James Brown. I seriously studied all his grooves. But in the early '70s these white boys in Oakland started a band called Tower of Power that caught my attention. No doubt they were as influenced by JB as me, but they put a different hurting on R&B. Their lead voice, Lenny Williams, was a soul-singing brotha, but the man who mattered to me most, the drummer, was a white dude, David Garibaldi.

David was different. Most drummers layer their dynamic, playing the high hat, snare, and kick simultaneously, creating a thick sound. Garibaldi took another approach. He had a linear style; he played one sound at a time. He made the drums sound like a precision machine with cogs fitting inside each other, pumping up and down, in and out. Almost like Whac-A-Mole. Smack one down into the hole and another pops up. He used phrases to create accent, not volume. Most jazz, rock, and R&B drummers fall into a consistent pattern with their right hand on the high hat or ride cymbal. Not Garibaldi. He was all over the place.

I became Garibaldi's student. I'd put on every Tower of Power record—especially songs like "Squib Cake" and "Oakland Stroke," where the drums are driving the controlled commotion—and play along. At first I just couldn't do it. Too hard. Too many moves. Too subtle. But damn if I didn't practice till I perfected that shit.

*U don't gotta go on about what a gr8 drummer u were.*

I ain't shy about saying that I worked it till I got it right.

That's funny, because as a kid I *was* shy. Didn't see myself as handsome. Didn't even see myself as cool. I was a freckle-faced kid who made no big impression. Wasn't no athlete. Wasn't no good student. All I had was music, and music was enough. Going to see the Jackson 5 took off the top of my head. The Beatles fascinated me. Loved Booker T and the M.G.'s, whose drummer Al Jackson Jr. had a pocket deep as the Grand Canyon.

*U best explain the pocket. Folk don't know what u b talkin' 'bout.*

The pocket comes at the back of the beat. Good funk never can anticipate the beat but lets the beat come to you. It's all about relaxation. Get up tight with time and time will fuck you up. Timing's everything, but time is nothing you can control. You gotta let it ride. Let it flow. Then follow that flow. More you put yourself behind that flow, more you can push that flow. Enter the flow. Be one with the flow.

So it was the musical flow that got me through all the ups and downs of my scrambled childhood. Mom had her own flow that most of the time took her out of the house. She had her gigs. She had her aspirations. She had her common sense that, after a year or so, told her to dump gangster Joe.

Mom was also a dreamer. Example: She had a notion that Minneapolis could support the biggest indoor mall in the world. It was a whole vision. She drew it all out on paper. There were diagrams and architectural renderings. Mom, who also wrote movie scripts and short stories, had this brilliance she wanted the world to recognize. She found a congressman who would listen to her and finally got a meeting with a real estate investor. He looked at her plans for the mall and didn't laugh. He gasped. He was all excited and said he could see exactly what she had in mind. He'd get back to her. He never did. Meanwhile, she hustled her way into the office of other investors but could never score. Fast-forward fifteen years to the opening of Mall of America, some 5.4 million square feet, built where Interstate 494 meets State Highway 77 just north of the Minnesota River. Biggest mall in the world. Huge success. Mom felt sure that her ideas had made it to the powers that be but they didn't need her.

Mom had dreams, and I love her for that. I think she implanted those dreams in me, though they didn't come up for a long time. And yet her dreams merged with my music in a way that I would never have imagined.

*Neither would I.*

# 3

# THE LUNCHROOM

When I was coming up, Minneapolis was not Atlanta or LA. By that I mean its black population was tiny. There was no chocolate city within the big city. Or if there was, it was a very thin slice of chocolate. Not sure if even 2 percent of Minneapolis–St. Paul was African American. The effect, I believe, was the creation of solidarity. There weren't many of us, so we knew to stick together. I personally didn't experience blatant racism. My brother, Jesse, was called names and I can recall a few episodes, but by and large we lived our lives in a pretty cool space.

On KQRS, the popular radio station, you might hear Three Dog Night followed by Bill Withers followed by the Rolling Stones. Herbie Hancock's Headhunters were in the air. So were the Doobie Brothers and Elton John. Folks in the hood were hooked on Al Green and Teddy Pendergrass. But generally no one drew strict lines between genres. White and black blended together. Compared, say, to Chicago or New York, the Twin Cities were chill. I'm not saying there wasn't deep-down racial tension. And I'm not saying that certain white folk didn't express attitudes of superiority. America is America. When jazz pianist Erroll Garner asked Louis Armstrong, "What's up,

Pops?," Armstrong's answer, "White folks are still ahead," spoke for all of us.

Exposure to a wide variety of music in a wide variety of genres informed my future at an early age.

*U might as well b talkin' 'bout me.*

I am. But in this story I still haven't met you.

*U heard us in the lunchroom. U called this chapter "The Lunchroom." Well, take us inside the lunchroom.*

I'm feeling like *you* wanna produce this book.

*All I'm sayin' is—if u want a hit book, then hit it! Get 2 it!*

I'll get it when I'm ready to get it. You don't even know how I wound up in the lunchroom.

*Does it even matter?*

To you it don't. To me it does. See, I didn't get there 'cause of you. I got there cause of a chick. She was fine, and I was trying to get next to her. She said something about a band she wanted to hear. She mentioned a Friday-night show up at Central High, your school. At the time I was at North High. The girl didn't mention you. She didn't even mention the name of your band. She just said there was music.

*But u had heard of me, right?*

That's another myth you made up in your mind. Truth is, I hadn't heard shit about you. At the time you were living with your mom in a house just down the street from us. Nice house too. A lot nicer than ours. But you being in that crib was something I learned later. When I walked into the lunchroom, I walked in cold. Didn't have a clue.

*& how'd u react?*

First, my visual impression of you was that huge Afro blown out to the max. Black turtleneck sweater, a pair of wacky bell-bottoms and pink woolen girl gloves with the fingers cut out so you could sting your guitar. That was my first glimpse of what I'd call your metrosexual vibe.

*Meaning what?*

Meaning most cats liked straight-up leather gloves. But you liked lady mittens and didn't care what anyone thought about it. You liked the flair of certain accessories, even if the flair was feminine.

*So u were worried 'bout my sexuality?*

Not worried and couldn't have cared less. I'd soon see you were straight as a gate. And even if you swung the other way, it wouldn't have mattered. All I'm saying is that there was a gender-bender side to you that came out early. You knew how to exploit it.

*Exploit sounds like a bad thing.*

Maybe *exploit*'s the wrong word. Maybe it was just you being you.

*& who was that?*

A badass musician looking to make waves and grab attention. A guitarist who, at fifteen, had absorbed all of Eric Clapton and thrown in Jeff Beck for good measure. Later I learned you'd even studied the cats that influenced Hendrix—Johnny Guitar Watson and Buddy Guy. Got the idea you'd been drinking in this music like babies drink in mama's milk.

*U'd been drinking some of that milk yourself.*

Not like you. I was a serious drummer. My chops were sharp. But I recognized you as a different breed of cat entirely. You didn't just play the fuckin' music. You *were* the fuckin' music. It consumed you, just like it consumed everyone who heard it. Never had seen anything like that before. That's why I wanted in.

I wanted in your band, Grand Central, but I wasn't in the "in crowd." I was standing outside watching you soaring on guitar, Terry Jackson on timbales, William Doughty on congas, André Anderson—later to change his name to André Cymone—on bass, André's sister Linda on keys, and drummer Charles "Chazz" Smith.

Chazz had the spot I wanted, but I'd been told Chazz was your cousin. Didn't matter that I could outplay him. I couldn't outmaneuver him.

The repertoire was heavy funk, lots of Sly and the Family Stone and Rufus, with everyone taking turns on vocals. You sang with a Chaka Khan–like fire. Your falsetto felt as strong as Curtis Mayfield's. The whole band rocked.

You were clearly the star, playing on a plateau high above everyone else. You were also distant. Not the kind of cat, even in high school, who could slide up to me and say, "Hey, man, whassup? Let's hang."

On the other hand, André *was* that kind of cat. He had an easygoing personality. He was all heart and super approachable. Like me, he liked weed and listening to advanced music. He'd play me Weather Report. I'd play him Return to Forever. We were deep into fusion. He studied bassist Jaco Pastorius. I studied drummer Billy Cobham. John McLaughlin and the Mahavishnu Orchestra. The Tony Williams Lifetime. We liked the far-out cats.

André and I tightened up and spent lots of time together. I still never mentioned how much I wanted to join Grand Central. Figured it was better to lay back in the cut. Then came the day André came over to my house. He noticed I'd set up my drum kit. For all our talk about music, I hadn't pushed my own agenda.

"You got the drums set up like you're serious," he said.

"I am."

"Play something."

I was ready. I threw a couple Tower of Power platters on the box—"What Is Hip?" and "Soul Vaccination." I played David Garibaldi's part to where there was no daylight between me and David. Brother, I had his part *down.*

"Why didn't you tell me?" asked André.

"Tell you what?"

"That you play your ass off."

I just smiled.

"You should come by band rehearsal."

"What for? Y'all got Chazz."

"We're having problems with Chazz. Come by and audition."

Music to my ears.

Week later, I was over at Terry Jackson's house. Rehearsal was in the basement. Chazz's drums were set up, but I arrived with my own kit. Part of me was nervous. Part of me excited. I had butterflies but also confidence. I'd spent thousands of hours home alone banging out some of the most complex drum patterns in modern music. I had this. I knew I did.

Everyone was friendly except Prince. Prince was cool. Standoffish.

*I didn't know what 2 expect. Didn't really know who u were.*

And you weren't about to make me feel comfortable. That wasn't your style. Your style was to challenge my chops. On the other hand, André was super supportive. His sister Linda gave out good vibes. The other cats were all smiles. But you weren't smiling. I'm not saying you were scowling, but I could feel your skepticism. You were looking down.

After I got through setting up, I signaled that I was ready to go. You called Sly's "Dance to the Music" and counted it off. No problem. I was there. I could pick the pocket of that song blindfolded, and I did. Felt great. Linda, André, and the boys gave me looks of approval. Nothing from you. You were playing and singing; you were deep into the groove I was grinding. After it was over, though, you didn't say a word.

You called another tune, "Evil Ways," that I knew from the Carlos Santana/Buddy Miles live record. Buddy was another monster drummer I'd been studying, so this groove wasn't new. I rode it right. Smooth sailing all the way. Everyone happy. Gotta presume you were happy 'cause you were calling off more tunes. I was there for every one of 'em. Funkadelic's "Free Your Mind and Your Ass Will Follow"? JB's "Get On the Good Foot"? I was on it.

On it for a couple of hours. Felt natural as breathing. When you finally called it a night, I got a couple of slaps on the back from the others but my man was still standoffish. You didn't even tell me goodbye.

"What does that mean?" I asked André the next day.

"Means you got the gig. Otherwise you'd hear he wasn't happy."

I was happy, not only because I was in a band I'd been dying to join but because I knew, in order to hang with these cats, I'd have to hone my chops. I was up for it. I had the vocal support of my bandmates except for Prince, who stayed silent. That was his way. Aloofness was how he stood apart. He led aloofly but intensely.

I never have—before or since—seen anyone work with music with his kind of focus. I could be on the clock for hours at a time. I thought I was devoted. But Prince, man, that motherfucker was never *off* the clock. He slept, ate, drank, and devoured music. Couldn't stop writing it, rehearsing it, performing it. He was possessed and remained that way every waking day.

*So u gonna admit I gave u that work ethic that got u thru?*

Admit it gladly. Admit it openly. Shout it from the mountaintop. Thank you, brother, for schooling me on what it means to do it tight and right. I know you had your own teachers. JB. Bootsy. Sly. But you took it further. You tightened it until it couldn't be tightened no more.

And in the meantime, we had fun.

*& created a sound. U better break down that birth of the sound. The birth of Minneapolis funk.*

You could probably explain better than me.

*It's your book, wiseass. U get 2 do the explainin'.*

I'd start out by saying that necessity was the mother of invention. We didn't have horns—couldn't afford them—so the keyboard was doing some of the lead lines. Linda was playing a Farfisa electric organ that, along with your guitar and André's bass, gave Grand Central a full-on funk effect different from other bands.

*U haven't talked about our competitors.*

You saw 'em as competitors. The rest of us saw 'em as brothers.

Jimmy Jam and Terry Lewis had a band called Flyte Time. And yes, they could fly. They got their name from the Donald Byrd funk/jazz jam "Flight Time" and their sound from a three-piece horn section.

Jimmy and Monte Moir, a bad white boy who sang soul, were great keyboard players, Terry a superb bassist, Jellybean Johnson a killer drummer and their first vocalist, Cynthia Johnson, a sista who could shout. (Jellybean, by the way, was, like me, left-handed. I always thought that made both our styles a little distinctive.)

Great as Flyte Time was, Prince was pushing us to be greater. Prince was pushing us to the edge. Over the edge. Gig after gig after gig. We played high school dances, VFW halls, and local clubs like the Riverview and Nacirema (that's *American* spelled backward). Sometimes there'd be battles of the bands with Flyte Time. Both bands were banging. A supersonic Prince guitar solo would win over the crowd, but then a Jimmy Jam fireworks display on keys would make 'em just as crazy.

Everyone was singing. William Doughty had a William Orange–style "Brick House" voice when we covered Commodores tunes. I sang Billy Preston's "Will It Go Round in Circles" and the deep blues ballad by Major Harris, "Love Won't Let Me Wait." I was feeling pretty good about my voice until Flyte Time hired Alexander O'Neal, who, hands down, was the heavyweight champ, Minneapolis's own Wilson Pickett. Talent was everywhere.

Interesting that the first adult to see this talent and act upon it was my beloved mother. Remember, Mom was a practical woman. She was not easily taken in or impressed. She looked at life realistically. When I started playing drums, she saw it as a lark. Just a little-kid hobby. When I got better, she still wasn't ready to say I had a future in music. But when she heard Grand Central, her whole attitude changed. She went to one show, and just to be sure she wasn't fooling herself, she went to another. And then another. After three or four Grand Central shows, Mom said it straight up: "Y'all aren't just good. You're fantastic. You deserve a deal. And I'm going to get you one."

Which was when things got crazy.

# 4
# GOOD TIMES

For the two years I played with Grand Central, it was a beautiful situation.

*Glad 2 hear u say that, bro. Wouldn't want no one 2 badmouth that band.*

Wouldn't dream of it. We were learning as we were gigging, growing as we were woodshedding, moving from wet-behind-the-ears kids to young pros who knew what it took to goose a crowd until no one sat for our set, no matter how long we played.

The typical Grand Central set was off the hook.

Might open with Earth, Wind & Fire's "Shining Star."

Then Prince would sing a couple of Rufus songs. He loved Chaka Khan and sang Chaka's leads with as much passion as Chaka herself. He'd tear up "Tell Me Something Good" and "Sweet Thing."

The Isley Brothers' "Fight the Power." Bootsy's Rubber Band's "Psychoticbumpschool." Funkadelic's "Get Off Your Ass and Jam." LTD's "Love Ballad." We were all fans of Jeffrey Osborne, LTD's lead singer. Sly's "Dance to the Music." And for sure "Ffun" by Con Funk Shun. In short, we were deep into fierce funk.

*U make it sound like we were a cover band.*

Just saying that the backbone of everything was funk. And funk wasn't anything we invented. The great inventors—from Chuck Berry through Bo Diddley to James Brown—'specially JB!—were our teachers and our gurus. We loved them. We found their funk so beautiful, so irresistible, so much fuckin' fun that we naturally copied the cats that came after Chuck and Bo and James. I'm talkin' 'bout Sly, the Isleys, Clinton, Bootsy, Cameo, Lakeside, Graham Central Station, Ohio Players, and all the others. So yes, we were a cover band. Like most bands, we started off covering stuff. And, yes, we did it to pay our respects to our elders. But there was another reason: We did it to survive. Surviving in those clubs meant getting the party people up and dancing. And you could only do that by playing hits they already knew from the radio.

*All true. But also true is that I always had originals.*

You did. But we had to sneak those originals in between the radio hits.

*My originals were just as good as anything on the radio.*

Okay, let me just stop and reestablish a fact that can't be reestablished enough. Everyone reading this must believe me when I say Prince possessed genius. Unprecedented genius. Think back to Elvis, the cat some folk say invented rock and roll. Elvis was cool. Elvis had a look. He sang. Worked his pelvis. Drove the girls crazy. Would never dis Elvis for borrowing from black music 'cause he publicly acknowledged his masters. He loved him some B. B. King. He respected Ray Charles. He covered Ray's songs. But if they call Elvis the King, they're gonna have to call Prince the World Emperor. I say that cause, unlike Prince, Elvis did not write. Elvis did not arrange. Elvis did not play killer guitar. And when I say that Prince wrote and arranged, I mean he wrote and arranged literally thousands of songs under so many different names that he forgot half of them. And when I say Prince played guitar, I mean he blended the styles of all the guitar gurus and then added a fantastic flair all his own. He did more than arrange. He created a sound that, nearly a half century later, sounds as fresh as it did when Grand Central was tearing the roofs off every school auditorium in the Twin Cities.

So I praise my brother without reservation. And will continue to praise him with the last breath in my body. However . . .

*Uh-oh. I don't like the sound of that "however." Here comes the bad part.*

No bad part. Just the fact that you cloaked yourself in mystery. Mystery was your protection. Mystery was your way of clutching control with an even tighter fist. Mystery was to you the way prayers are to priests. You couldn't live without mystery. Couldn't operate without it. You had your own clock—your own timetable and agenda—and no one but you was allowed to see it.

Prince was serious, but Prince was also funny. The way I finally broke through his heavy armor was with humor. He liked to laugh and, in that way, wasn't all that different from the Minneapolis brothas who loved pulling pranks and cracking jokes. Prince talked street talk; he chopped it up with as much salt and swag as anyone.

His lighthearted vibe was great, but it came with limits. Prince could shut it down in a hot second. And when he did, when the joking ended, brotha would slip back into his Mystery Man pose. That pose was his fallback. What it said was "You don't really know me; no one does, and no one knows what I'm going to do next."

*There u go, trying 2 understand what u can't understand.*

I understand more than you want me to understand. I understand that you used mystery. But I want to say that I respect the mystery. It worked. Helped make you a motherfuckin' superstar. All hail Mystery Man!

When Prince and I first started hanging, he was living with his mother, Mattie, and sister Tyka down the street from us. Mattie had divorced Prince's dad—John Lewis Nelson (who, as a musician, also called himself Prince)—and married Hayward Baker. Mattie and Hayward had a son, Omarr. There was a piano in the basement, where Prince started experimenting. Prince and his stepdad had their problems. Big-time tension. Mattie was a pretty lady who didn't say much. She'd been a jazz singer and gigged with Prince's dad, John.

Because Prince and Hayward wasn't cool, Prince busted a move, leaving Mattie's crib for John's, way across Olson Highway. Like father, like son. John was also a very aloof cat. You never knew what he was thinking. Reminded me of Vincent Price. John was also a serious musician. Prince was proud of his dad, who constructed far-out stuff. Avant-garde spacey jazz. But if you listened closely, you'd catch a melody line. You'd catch a groove. John was deep into his music.

When Prince moved out of his mom's place, he figured it'd be easier to deal with his real dad than his stepdad. From what I saw, though, that wasn't the case. John called Prince "Skipper," pronounced "Skippa." John was strict.

"Skippa," he said, "this is my house and you best live by my rules."

"Skippa," he warned, "if you ain't home by 11, don't bother to come home."

"Skippa," he gave notice, "if I catch you with one of your little girlfriends up in here, I'll put your ass out."

Which brings up another subject.

Girls.

*Don't say more than u really know.*

I know what I know. I know that you loved playing sports, but, man, you also loved the ladies. Music first. Music always first. But the fair sex second. Girls buzzed around your pint-sized ass like bees around honey. Of course it helped—it helped all of us—that we were musicians playing sexy music. Helped that you was always fresh and clean. You knew how to dress. A small army of chicks saw you as drop-dead handsome. Your mysterious aura had a powerfully sensuous side. You was a playa who played by keeping the cards close to your chest. That applied to everything in your life. No one was gonna check you. Not even your dad.

Funny part was if I had to say whose personality Prince most resembled, I'd say his father. Two hardheaded cats bound to bump heads. Don't think Prince was living at John's for more than six months when John made good on his threat: He kicked his son out for bringing girls over to the crib. That's when Prince moved to André's basement.

The band liked that move 'cause it gave us more time to jam. For most folk, getting kicked out of the crib by Daddy is a traumatic thing. Maybe it was for Prince; maybe he was angry and furious, but I never heard him say a word except "Let's rehearse an extra two hours tonight."

Mom had bought me a little four-track recorder that Prince would use to lay down his ideas. That was fine with us. What wasn't fine was when he'd show up at all hours, banging on the door, saying he had to get in to record a song that had just flown into his head. Sometimes we let him in, and sometimes—like the night he wanted to barge in at 3 a.m.—we'd try to ignore him. But damn if he wouldn't stop banging. Rather than let him bust down the door, I'd get out of bed, let the brotha in, and help him lay down the track. On other nights I'd just turn off the lights and let him bang. I was just too damn tired to make music.

*Or stoned.*

Oh, hell, yes. Which brings up another point: Prince didn't do drugs. I wasn't a heavy drug user in high school. I just liked weed. Weed provided a filter that mellowed me out while intensifying the music. And of course weed is a potent aphrodisiac. If you have to choose between making love high or sober, high wins every time. To Prince's credit, he bucked the culture. He stayed clean. He stayed clean to stay in shape. He loved playing sports, especially hoop. He didn't need that extra creative boost that marijuana provides. He didn't need that elevation. He could get to the higher plateau without stimulants. He was that good.

I also think Prince feared drugs, and with good reason, 'cause drugs undercut control. Prince needed control at all times. He didn't want his vision clouded or his mind altered. His hyperactive mind didn't require any further hype. He knew where he wanted to go and how to get there.

That put him at odds with my mother. Mom was thorough and deliberate. Prince was impetuous and impatient. For a while, though, he accepted her as our manager. That's because no one but Mom funded us to go into a studio to cut demos. No one but Mom spent her own bread to fly to New York and meet with record execs to try to seal a deal. No one but Mom made sure we had rehearsal space. Mom was also always upbeat and encouraging, assuring us that it was only a matter of time before we'd get our big-time break.

*Your mama never did what she said she'd do.*

Last thing you wanna do is go talkin' 'bout my mom. Mom was gutsy. She was fearless. She wrangled her way into meetings with high-powered record men. She called CEOs and chairmen of the board. She forced her way into the offices of A&R cats. She had a one-on-one with Isaac Hayes, who dug our demo tape and promised to hook us up. But all this took time. You were impatient. So on the side you started dealing with a dude named Owen Husney who owned a local ad agency. Husney even got you to do a jingle for a ladies' clothing shop called GG's.

What we didn't know was that Husney had been shopping a record deal for you in Los Angeles. And we heard he got Warner Brothers interested based on a tape that you gave him. And that the tape was made by us—Grand Central—but the label thought it was you playing all the instruments.

*I could have if I'd wanted 2.*

That ain't the point. Sure you could have. But you didn't. You got a solo deal with Grand Central demos. You'd given up on trying to get the band signed. You lost patience with Mom. She was still out there looking to score for Grand Central when we found out that you had already scored—without us.

In the grand scheme of things, this was a brilliant move. Most of your moves were brilliant. You saw solo Prince as a better vehicle than Grand Central. You wanted a new kind of sound. You wanted to give your funk a New Wave edge and a New Wave look. It was post-punk time. The Police, the Cars, the Cure, Boy George, and Bowie. You had a worldwide vision that didn't include Grand Central.

I only wish you had clued us in on your vision. Instead, you said nothing. Just disappeared, leaving us to scramble.

Grand Central without Prince was like Desi without Lucy.

So time for a Princeless chapter.

This chapter turned out rough.

# 5

# SHAMPAYNE

Strange spelling, but that was the name of our new band.

> *I'd shown u that strange spelling was an attention-getter. I'd shown u how being normal gets u nowhere.*

You showed me a lot of shit. After you split, I tried to use that shit to keep us going. We were convinced we could make it without you. We should have known better. But we were young and hungry. Between all of us switching off, we had vocal power. We had musical power. Yet with you gone, we'd lost our star power. During rehearsals, we weren't as tough on ourselves as you'd been on us. We'd lost our leader.

Then when we lost André Cymone, we really found ourselves sputtering. No one could blame André for accepting an offer to join your new band. If I'd been given that offer, I would've grabbed it. But no offer came. You didn't see me as part of your immediate musical future. Warner Brothers had given you a deal and you were gearing up to cut your first album.

Shampayne fizzled out.

I was despondent. I was also drifting. I'd dropped out of North High after my junior year and hadn't developed any skills beyond music. While my music had tapered off, my love life hadn't. I'd fallen for a young attractive woman, Jennifer Graves, who, on October 17, 1975, gave birth to our precious daughter, Tionna. I was eighteen. I lacked the maturity and responsibility that fatherhood required. But I loved this little girl and wanted to do right by her.

The problem was that I had no real direction. The strongest element in my life remained Mom. As a go-getter, she never slowed down. And seeing that I was having a hard time keeping myself together, she came up with a solution. She bought herself a brand-new 1977 maroon T-top Grand Prix and we moved to Maryland. Sandy stayed in Minneapolis and Jesse went to live with his dad in Illinois. It was just Mom and me. The plan was to bring out Jennifer and Tionna once we got settled.

Mom chose Gaithersburg, halfway between Baltimore and D.C., because we could move in with her best friend, Francis. Meanwhile, she could easily travel up the coast to New York and continue to try to land me a record deal. I had made other demos that, at least in my mind, were as good as the demo Prince had used to nail his Warner Brothers contract. At the same time, I had no illusions. I was not Prince. I could not play every instrument and I could not sing or write with his facility. But I could play drums, I could play a little keyboards, a little guitar, I could sing, I could write, and I had a mother who wasn't about to give up on me.

Mom worked in a beauty-supply store selling wigs before getting a good government gig at the Opportunities Industrialization Center as a job development specialist. Count on Mom to land on her feet. Count on me to keep floundering. Odd jobs here and there hardly satisfied my musical soul, so I found myself moving into a jazz community of serious players. All my friends were jazz cats. I sat in with all kinds of bands. There was no money in it but lots of artistic satisfaction—not to mention growth. I was aware of the history of jazz drumming. I knew about Basie's big band drummers Papa Jo Jones and Sonny Payne. I knew about Louie Bellson and Buddy Rich. But until Maryland I'd never played straight-up bop in the style of Art Blakey and Max Roach. I was proud to become a decent jazz drummer who could hold his own with the heavyweight players in the D.C. area. But besides an occasional gig, my money was still funny.

Mom chipped in, helping me rent an apartment for Jennifer and Tionna in the same complex where we were staying. For a while, that boosted my spirits. But the boost didn't last long. Young as we were, Jennifer and I got in each other's way. The relationship collapsed under the weight of my unhappiness. Jennifer and our daughter soon moved back to Minneapolis. I never gave Tionna the time and care she deserved.

There was a moment when my misery came to a head. I managed to find work at Montgomery Ward, where they put me behind the counter of their rental-car division.

"Would you like a green Ford Pinto or an orange Chevy Vega?" I'd ask the customer.

I wasn't happy.

One of my coworkers, Tyrel, had a boom box that he'd bring to the gig. Fine with me. These were disco days, when Donna Summer was calling out "Last Dance," Gloria Gaynor was declaring "I Will Survive," the Jacksons were ready to "Blame It on the Boogie," and Rick James was firing up "Mary Jane." I dug it all.

Wasn't until I heard a song called "Soft and Wet," though, that I spun around and listened hard.

*There I was.*

Yes, sir. It was you. On the radio! Prince! That voice, that snappy groove, that distinctively dirty Minneapolis funk. Being driven insane by a certain body part he called "soft and wet." Sex-obsessed, Prince had cut a track not unlike dozens of the tracks we had cut together.

"That's my boy," I told Tyrel. "We played in a band together."

"Sure you did, Morris."

"Really, man, I was the drummer. He's my homeboy. Prince. That's him."

Tyrel looked at me like I was out of my head.

"If you were such a solid drummer," he said, "what you doing here renting out Impalas?"

Didn't have an answer. So I simply sulked.

I went to the record store to see an actual copy of Prince's first album, *For You.* I shelled out $6.98 to buy it. Had to hear it all. What I heard was that Prince had refined the sound he'd started to sculpt with Grand Central. He was playing all the instruments, and playing the hell out of them. The songs were a little slicker than what he'd been writing before, but the funk was firmly in place. He was clearly going for that pop feeling that was sweeping the clubs from London to LA.

I went to the newsstand to grab a *Billboard* and see how the record was selling. "Soft and Wet" was a little bit of a hit on the R&B charts, but the second single, "Just as Long as We're Together," didn't go nowhere. Neither crossed over. I know that didn't make Prince happy. Prince loved him some R&B—Prince *was* R&B—but Prince was flat-out determined to get beyond the R&B market. That's true of virtually every black artist who ever sang.

Do the math. If blacks comprise 12 percent of the population and even a smaller percent of the wealth, where's the big money? Crossover. That's the name Ray Charles gave his own label after he had huge crossover hits like "Georgia on My Mind" and "I Can't Stop Loving You." That's what Chuck Berry had in mind when he tailored his lyrics to white bobby-soxers.

I'm not saying Prince compromised his music. What I am saying is that he aimed his music at the widest audience possible. He was shrewd in the same way Nat King Cole, Sam Cooke, and Sly Stone had been shrewd. The wider the appeal, the better.

The title cut, "For You," shows off his ability to harmonize his own voices, à la Marvin Gaye, only he puts it in an almost classical bag, introducing himself to the world as a different kind of artist. When he drops the groove, the mood changes and the song radiates a Chic-like charm. He doesn't "Freak Out" completely, but he sure knows what's happening on the dance floor in urban America.

*U thru explaining what I had in mind?*

I dig my explanation. You don't?

*Not saying. Never thought it smart 2 explain my music. Leave it 2 others 2 say what it means 2 them.*

Well, I'm sure enough one of the "others." And I'm saying I dug it. I saw that your whole operation was off and running. The album cover showed you literally coming out of the shadows. It wasn't a clear photo. It caught you on the run. It only showed your face. It was also a little blurry, but it was definitely a statement saying that you were here. And I wanted to be there with you. Oh, brother, did I want to be there with you!

*Y didn't u come back 2 Minneapolis? I was there.*

Guess I was too down to think straight. Minneapolis would have made sense 'cause Jennifer and Tionna were there. Reconciliation with loved ones always makes sense. But I wasn't ready for that. I was seeing myself as a loser, a guy in a jive-ass Montgomery Ward blazer filling out rental forms for impatient customers. Mom and I were living in motels and raunchy apartments overlooking garbage dumpsters. I was in the dumps.

Seeing my distress, Mom came up with a plan. Mom always had a plan. California dreaming, she suggested we leave Maryland and head to San Jose, where her cousin Regina had moved after she and Spike had divorced. Funny, but Regina, who had originally drawn us to Minneapolis, was now drawing us to San Jose.

Big mistake. I hated it. Hated how Aunt Regina's domestic situation had forced her into a three-bedroom apartment with nine people. Hated my gig as a salesman in a men's store at the mall. Hated trying to talk cats into buying shitty clothes they didn't want.

Switching jobs just made things worse. I got on a construction cleanup crew. I swung a sledgehammer breaking stucco off the base of new homes, picked up the pieces, and hauled 'em to some smelly landfill. Did that for a month until my back said no more. But a man's gotta work so I thought life would be easier as a security guard. Applied, was accepted and issued a shiny-new blue uniform. Badge and everything.

The night before my first day on the job, I couldn't sleep. Tossing and turning, I thought my brain would explode. What was I doing living with Mom and Aunt Regina in a place where every morning the line to the bathroom was agonizingly long? What was I doing taking menial jobs when, in fact, I did have a skill I'd been working on since I was a kid? I could do music. None of the music I heard on the radio intimidated me. It inspired me and made me realize that, as good as Shalamar's "Take That to the Bank" might be, I could have provided the rhythm for that track. I didn't want to live my life like the line that Marlon Brando, a boxer forced to throw a fight, says to his brother in *On the Waterfront*: "I could've been a contender."

I had to get back into the ring. Had to get back to Minneapolis. Jennifer was calling. Tionna was crying for me. And Prince, only months after his first record had dropped, came out with another, simply called *Prince*. This time he was out of the shadows. The cover showed him full-on shirtless with "Prince" written in purple script above his wavy shoulder-length hair. And this time his music did cross over. "I Wanna Be Your Lover" charted high on pop radio. He'd done what he'd set out to do—reach the masses.

Now I had to do the only thing that made sense: head home.

# 6

# DRUMMER FOR HIRE

Big sis Sandy was always like my second mother, so it's no surprise that I moved in with her as soon as I returned to Minneapolis. I visited my baby, Tionna, but my relationship with Jennifer was still raw. I wanted to get back with my daughter and her mom, but I didn't have the means to support them. I couldn't even support myself.

I did, though, make a vow: Support would have to come from music. I'd taken enough low-paying, soul-crushing jobs. Maybe I wasn't Tony Williams, but I *was* a drummer, I *was* a musician, and I promised myself to stay on that track. That meant freelancing, playing behind any Twin Cities band that would have me. Jazz, R&B, cocktail lounges, high school dances, bar mitzvahs. Didn't matter. I was going to make money making music, no matter how thin they sliced the bread.

Because the black music scene in Minneapolis is small, it didn't take long to see my old running buddies. Flyte Time was getting even more gigs since, with the demise of Grand Central and Shampayne, the competition had dwindled. Word was that Prince had not abandoned Minneapolis. In fact, he never would. He had formed a new band and started rehearsing in the burbs south of the city.

"You should come by," said André Cymone, who was playing bass in the band. "Prince would love to see you."

I was a little hesitant. André had told me that Bobby Z, a white boy, was the drummer. I knew I could outplay him, but I also knew that a salt-and-pepper lineup was important to Prince. He saw it as another way to facilitate crossover.

Sensing my hesitation, André urged me on.

"There's a lot happenin' 'round Prince right now," he said. "You should be part of it. Why don't you ride out there with me?"

A week later I took him up on the offer. Walking in with André, Prince's main man, would make things easier. It was a fall afternoon. The leaves were turning crazy gold and red, the sky a brilliant blue, a mild breeze blowing through the burbs. I was more excited than anxious. It'd be good to see Prince. It'd been too long.

When we arrived, he was already there, guitar in hand. He looked at me and didn't exactly beam, but he didn't scowl. I thought I saw him break into a small smile.

*U saw right. Didn't hold no grudges. Wasn't anything 2 hold a grudge about.*

But was *I* holding a grudge? Was *I* pissed that it was the Grand Central demo that had nailed the Warner Brothers deal? Was *I* pissed that I wasn't named the drummer of this hot new band the Revolution? If I was pissed, I decided being pissed would do me no good. So I chilled. Stayed friendly. Said I was happy to help any way I could.

*U were 2 smart 4 that. U understood the train was leaving the station & u wanted on the train.*

I got on the train.

Prince's second album was outstripping his first by leaps and bounds. I was eager to be part of the phenomenon.

And I was relieved that Prince welcomed me into his inner circle. He seemed genuinely glad to see me. Things picked up where they'd left off. He didn't have to ask whether I dug his first two albums. He knew I did. He didn't have to ask whether I was jonesing to get behind the drums. He knew I was. He also knew that I was a cat who could crack him up. The jokes came fast and furious. The brothas were back in action.

When his new band actually started to play, I saw how he was putting a new kind of hurting on pop-soul-funk. In the new songs he'd written for his third album, sex was even more prominent. And freakier.

During a break he came over to me to ask a question. I thought the question was gonna be "Wanna sit in on drums?" but it was something else entirely.

*U know how 2 work a video camera?*

That was the question. And my answer came quick: "I can learn in a hurry."

And brotha, I did.

Just like that, I became his videographer, lugging around a heavy-ass VHS cassette machine. But I'm not complaining.

*U got no reason 2. I kept u on the scene. Kept u in the mix.*

That's what I wanted. The camera brought me closer to the action, and the action was all about Prince. Because Prince liked being videotaped, my new job gave me more access to him than I'd ever had. I could move around as I pleased. The closer I got to him, the happier he was. Prince loved close-ups. He also loved having his daring dance moves and dramatic guitar gestures filmed so he could study them later. And, man, did he study them! He was a perfectionist. He dissected his every motion to make sure it was right. And if it wasn't, he'd rework it until it was.

He slowly came to rely on me for honest appraisals. Because I'd come up with him, I knew his stuff as well as anyone—with the possible exception of André. But André, being an especially gracious man, was more diplomatic than me. If I thought a song or a dance move was hokey, I'd let Prince know. He appreciated my candor and began relying on me as someone who'd speak my mind. So when it was time to go on tour, he took me along. I not only videotaped every show but had the freedom to critique. Prince was for anything that would improve his presentation.

The presentation was starting to include more of that metrosexual stuff. It wasn't enough for Prince to make sex a central theme in his music. He also wanted to use sex as a visual stimulant in his show. Like all stars, he wanted the attention on himself. That ain't unusual. But it was unusual as hell when he started to rock long coats with nothing on underneath except his undies. That sure as hell got everyone's attention. Provocative songs plus provocative outfits equals notoriety. Prince was looking to be notorious.

I was there for the Prince Tour, his first national go-round. It started in big clubs where he was the marquee name. Didn't have to open for anyone. Because he was getting all kinds of publicity, he could fill the Roxy in LA and the Capri Ballroom in Atlanta. The sex bit was big. More and more he was selling himself as a sex symbol, and the girls, white and black, were buying into it. Meanwhile, he kept developing material for his third album, *Dirty Mind*. No doubt he was intent on getting dirtier. A year before the record was released, he began to perform "Head," the story of a virgin on her way to her wedding. The singer hits on her, gives her head, comes all over her wedding dress, and winds up marrying her himself. Caused a helluva stir—which was just what Prince wanted.

Back then, *head* was the go-to term for oral sex. I remember Marvin Gaye using it a few years earlier on "Soon I'll Be Loving You Again" from his *I Want You* album. Marvin sang it hesitatingly. His generation of black men saw it as a forbidden act. The woman was supposed to sexually serve the man, not vice versa. But Marvin, who admits in the song that he's never done it before, talks himself into it, saying he'll do it soon while calling out the name of his wife, Janis.

Prince took a bolder approach. No hesitation. Didn't matter that the chick was promised to another cat. Didn't matter that she was a virgin. Those facts only added to the heat. More than his predecessors, Prince was ready to go down, get down, and stay down until every last female fan was satisfied.

By the end of the club portion of the Prince tour, "Head" was part of the show, and the audience, to make a terrible pun, was eating it up. I had it all on camera. Every night after the show, Prince would study his performance. No doubt he got off on himself—as most artists do—but he also admonished himself when he found fault. He knew when a dance move was wrong or a note off-key.

Fever was building to the point that the lines outside these clubs were snaking around the block. Frustrated fans were being turned away from sold-out shows. Prince needed bigger venues. And in 1979 going into 1980, the cat commanding the biggest venues was Rick James.

It was a mighty moment—Prince opening for Rick James. A torch was being passed. But the handoff was messy. Funny, but it was the same kind of mess Rick talked about when he got the torch handed off from the funk master before him, George Clinton. Clinton was seven years older than Rick, who felt George's resentment. Rick was ten years older than Prince, who felt Rick's resentment. In 1979, when they met up, Rick was 31, Prince 21, and yours truly, Prince's trusty videographer, 22.

Prince agreed to open for Rick's Fire It Up Tour. Rick was blazing hot. His *Fire It Up* album was burning up the charts with smashes like "Love Gun." Rick was at his peak, the cover photo showing him standing tall in tight thigh-high leather boots. Blowing smoke from a big blunt and sporting a white cowboy hat, he came on as King Rick.

With Rick commanding the mountaintop and Prince on the rise, it should have been the perfect pairing. It was anything but. The competition was nasty and the generation gap wide. First off, Rick was the ultimate stoner. He brandished his onstage joint the way Luke Skywalker brandished his lightsaber. Prince was straight-up sober. Not only did he not get high, he hated anyone getting high around him. I kept my weed away from the boss. Rick blew the shit in Prince's face. He used dope as his fuel while Prince was driven by pure energy.

The tour wound its way across the country for over three months, selling out the Omni in Atlanta and the Cobo Arena in Detroit. Started out great. I set up my JVC videocassette recorder on a tripod placed in the soundboard to get the best view of the stage.

Prince came out smokin'—not literally but figuratively. "Soft and Wet" was usually the opener. He'd also go into "I Feel for You," a song off his second album that, a few years later, Chaka Khan would turn into a smash cover. (It was beautiful to see an artist who Prince had covered so frequently in the Grand Central days actually singing *his* songs.) He'd squeeze "Head" somewhere into the set. Sexual innuendos flew from one side of the stage to the other. He began sporting his androgynous getup: the open trench coat revealing black leggings and bikini underwear. In 1979 that took balls. But Prince was Prince. He stepped on out and did what he wanted to do. The crowds went nuts. The press started saying that he was outstripping Rick.

Rick resented that. Later he wrote that the crowd booed when they saw Prince in his "bloomers." I didn't hear any boos on that tour. Rick also wrote about a drum battle between him and Prince, when supposedly Rick kicked Prince's ass. I knew nothing about that. I did know, though, that Rick started accusing Prince of stealing his licks and stage moves. I thought the accusation was silly.

We all steal. The line of musical thieves is endless, from Chuck Berry to Little Richard to Ike Turner to Jackie Wilson to Ray Charles to Stevie Wonder to Michael Jackson. If you don't like the word *steal*, then let's just say *borrow*. No matter how you look at it, though, every musical style is built on a previous style. Sure, there are innovators. All the artists I just mentioned are innovators. But innovations are based on shit that came before. That's what makes the innovations of these geniuses so startling. All at once, they contain past, present, and future.

Personality-wise, Rick and Prince were cut from similar cloth. They were hardly humble. *Arrogant* is a better word. They were musical visionaries, and they knew it. Rick had created a persona for himself—a larger-than-life character—and Prince was in the process of doing the same. Prince was looking for validation from Rick, and vice versa. Musically, the rivalry probably brought out the best in both men. Personally, they could have offered one another respect, but at least there was no bloodshed. The promoters cashed in on the conflict. As word of Prince's prowess grew, they renamed the tour the Battle of Funk.

*Looking back, who would u name the winner of that battle?*

There you go, tripping again. Do I gotta name you the winner? Do I gotta give you a gold medal for besting Rick? You got enough medals. Better to give Rick props. His contributions to funk were original. His roots in fusion and jazz were deep. Like you, Rick was a world-class writer, arranger, instrumentalist, and singer. Rick deserves recognition.

*If u say so.*

I do.

At the end of the tour, Prince no longer needed Rick. He was ready to go out on his own, but before he did he had to complete his third album. While he was working in the studio, he let me cut some tracks of my own. Big breakthrough. I guess I'd paid my dues. I had videotaped without complaining. I'd done what was asked of me. And of course all the time Prince knew how badly I wanted to get to the music. So at the end of the Fire It Up Tour he rewarded me with free use of his studio. My brotha was challenging me.

I jumped at the chance. I was determined to search my soul for the baddest groove in the history of bad grooves. Man, I was on it. Spent hours behind the drums until I found the stroke I knew would turn Prince inside out. Keep in mind, during these two years that I'd been behind the camera, I'd been studying his every move. At this point I knew his sound as well as he did. Plus I had some pretty damn good percussive ideas of my own.

Now, Prince was always cool, so when I presented him with a dance track I thought was hot, I didn't expect him to break out in applause. In fact, he didn't. But he did listen intently all the way through, nodding slightly. When he asked me to run it back from the top, I knew I was gold. He dug it. At the same time, he wouldn't commit to cutting it. Said we'd talk the next day.

Twenty-four hours later we were back in the studio when he said that he wanted the track. Bingo! But then a wrinkle: He said I had two options—he'd buy the song for $10,000 cold cash, or he could use it and I could get a record deal of my own. My choice. Naturally I chose the record deal.

A few weeks later, when Prince flew off to LA, he let me stay in his house in the Minneapolis burbs. I noticed a VHS tape in his recorder without a label. As his tape man, I labeled everything. What could this be? I slipped it in and saw that someone else had recorded Prince playing and dancing to my track. He'd completed it with a melody married to a set of lyrics called "Party Up." My fully fleshed-out track was untouched, only augmented by his vocal. The song, a declaration of his "revolutionary rock and roll," called the party people to the dance floor even as my man slipped in a political message about the futility of war. It was great.

Took a while for Prince to fulfill his promise. But I was a patient man. I was finally where I wanted to be. I was on the inside looking out. For a while I got back with Jennifer. I loved being with my daughter, but when it was time to hit the road I had to run. The road will kill any romance.

Prince had completed *Dirty Mind*, with "Party Up" as one of the eight songs. Prince owned it outright. The album read that everything was "produced, arranged, composed and performed by Prince." Not a word about my having written the track for "Party Up."

*That's the deal we made.*

Right. Which was why I never brought it up again. Also kept cool 'cause I still had hopes of being your drummer, but it wasn't meant to be. Instead I held on to the hope that I'd soon have my own record deal. Rather than rock the boat, I agreed to go back out on the road as your videographer during the Dirty Mind Tour. I could be humble if I had to.

There was always a method to Prince's madness. On his first album cover he was just moving out of the shadows; on the second he was shirtless; and on the third—*Dirty Mind*—he was in the trench coat pulled open to show his belly button and black bikinis. The look he'd tried out onstage was now officially imprinted on his latest musical offering. Some critics and fans pushed back, but I always admired him for not giving a fuck. This was the impression he wanted to make. He was a radical musical revolutionary, and that was that.

# 7

# EVOLUTION OF A REVOLUTION

I want to talk about Michael Jackson.

*U have 2?*

I want to because with the benefit of history we can look back and see two different major musicians moving on similar but different tracks.

*Y compare us?*

'Cause the comparison's fascinating. It's amazing to me that two geniuses hit their stride at just about the same time. Two master-blasters dominated the scene for decades. Also two of my biggest influences. Two of practically everyone's biggest influences.

Of course Michael came first. Prince and I heard the J5 when we were eleven years old. Michael was our age. We related. The songs—"ABC," "The Love You Save," "I Want You Back," "I'll Be There"—slayed us. Michael sang his ass off, and the tracks were off the chain. It was dance music, it was soul music, it was new music that turned Sly Stone's newfangled psychedelic funk in a new direction. We saw that our little preteen girlfriends liked it even more than we did.

They had J5 posters plastered all over their rooms. Everyone was caught up in Jacksonmania.

What we didn't know was that Michael didn't write or produce this material. He sang it. Berry Gordy had put together a Motown team of tunesmiths who created the sound. The Jackson 5 were stars, but they were also hired hands. That began to change when the Jacksons left Motown for Columbia and Michael started spreading his wings. He saw that he could also write and produce. That led to 1979, the year that he teamed up with Quincy Jones and turned out *Off the Wall*, the same year that Prince hit big with "I Wanna Be Your Lover" on his second album. Two twenty-one-year-old supertalented artists, born within two months of each other, coming out the gate with killer records that set the world on fire.

The differences, though, are profound. Michael's record was slicker. Where he once had Berry Gordy, now he had Quincy Jones, a master producer intent on polishing the discoish gloss to a high sheen. I'm not putting it down. I loved it.

Meanwhile, Prince didn't have a producer. Prince *was* the producer. Quincy was working with seamless disco grooves; Prince was working with grooves he'd developed back in the Grand Central days, grooves he now was refining with a sparser New Wave feel.

Boosted by their late-'70s successes, Michael and Prince stormed into the '80s. Nothing would stop them now. In '81, Prince hit with *Controversy*, where the sex was even more barefaced in songs like "Jack U Off." A year later *Thriller* broke the bank, another masterpiece of pop-soul where, although Michael wrote some of the songs, the album's greatness owed much to Quincy's musical vision. Over the coming years, Michael would break away from Quincy, using younger cutting-edge producers like Teddy Riley. But Prince remained Prince. He did it alone.

I'm not calling one better than the other. No matter how you break it down, genius is genius. But the genius that directly drove me to outdo myself—and even try to outdo him—was Prince. My education was in the do-it-yourself Minneapolis R&B scene, where less was more. Keep the funk lean and mean; let the synth sizzle; let the guitars scream; let the bass pop; drop the groove hard and heavy; never let up.

That's what I did on "Party Up," and that's what Prince did when he cut the song on *Dirty Mind*. On the strength of that album he was asked to open for the Rolling Stones. That was a big deal.

Along with the Beatles, the Stones define white rock-and-roll royalty. Their music is born out of black blues, and they've often given their opening slot to black acts. Mick was a Prince fan, and so, during the Stones' Tattoo You Tour in October 1981 at the Los Angeles Coliseum, the stage was set for Prince's next critical crossover move.

Mick might not have known it, but he was part of Prince's pantheon. It wasn't his rhythmic vibe that impressed Prince, although Keith Richards's licks and Charlie Watts's beat were nothing to sneeze at. Prince put Mick on a pedestal because of Mick's showmanship. He studied Mick's way of commanding the stage. He dug Mick's moves, his swagger, his rooster strut, his androgyny. David Bowie was also in Prince's mind mix, but Mick loomed larger 'cause the Stones played the biggest stadiums from Boston to Brazil. And if Prince liked anything, he liked big. He also liked the idea of exposing himself—his music as well as his body—to a whole new world of hard-core white rock and rollers. He was sure they'd love him.

He was sure wrong.

From my vantage point at the soundboard, with the video camera on its tripod, I shot the whole thing—the crowd booing Prince, throwing garbage at him, calling him a pussy. The reaction was so raucous that he couldn't even make it through the set. The rock fans ran him off the stage. It didn't help that he was wearing his trench coat/black bikini underwear outfit. Mick might have come on as sexually fluid in the late '70s, but in the early '80s Stones Nation was in a different place. The bikers and rockers wanted their jams uncut and unambiguous. Give it to 'em straight.

Prince was unprepared and shocked. This was to be his big moment. Just as his opening set had outshone Rick James, he was sure he could outshine the Stones. When I got to the dressing room, Prince was shaken to his core. Hadn't ever seen him like this.

"Doesn't mean shit," I said to him. "This crowd doesn't get it. But they will. And soon."

I kept strengthening his spirits 'cause I knew he needed that.

*I did. & I thank u. Think I even bought u a new Mustang.*

Wasn't new. It was a '79. But I was grateful.

*& I was grateful for your support.*

My support was sincere. You were misunderstood and that pissed me off. I saw you for who you were—a progressive artist way ahead of your time. Or at least ahead of the mob that showed up for the Stones.

"You're the only one with the guts to go out wearing the shit you wanna wear," I said.

I kept encouraging him 'cause I saw my words were landing. At first he talked about not even going out there the second night of this two-night gig. But by evening's end his mood had turned and the next day he reappeared onstage. Same outfit. Same songs. There were some boos, but fewer. This time he stood his ground and completed the set. Couldn't call it a triumph—the applause was scattered—but I could see that Prince demonstrated that steely determination that, despite this minor stumble, would keep his career soaring.

Prince had the Revolution but he wanted more. He wanted a stable of artists that he could produce. He wrote so many songs that he couldn't possibly sing them all. He had so many ideas for musical productions that he couldn't execute them all. He needed a whole team to express his artistry. He also wanted to make a shitload of money, and the more acts he owned, the more he'd make.

He kept his promise about getting me a record deal. But it wasn't the deal I'd imagined. I was a little disappointed because I had played drums on two of the jams from his upcoming *Controversy* album—the title tune and "Let's Work"—and I could tell he was pleased. If he hadn't been, I would have heard about it right quick.

But he didn't see me filling the slot as a solo artist. He wanted me to put together a band. I had no problem with that. I've always been a band guy. Solo stardom had never been my obsession as it was for Prince. A band would be beautiful. A band would let me finally get behind the drums and play my heart out.

*I knew it'd make u happy.*

It did, brotha.
At least for a while.

# 8

# TIME FOR THE TIME

*Tell 'em how I got u on the charts.*

You just gotta chill. You still rushing me. I need to dish out some background info first.

*Don't u think we've had enough background info? Time 2 jump from the verse 2 the hook.*

I'll be quick.

Because being videographer wasn't paying all my bills, I supplemented my income by gigging as a drummer for a local outfit with the enticing name of Enterprise Band of Pleasure. Once you worked for Prince, though, he had a thing about you working, even part-time, for anyone else. Prince looked to own you.

*Overstatement. Prince liked 2 help u.*

Prince liked to get credit for helping me. But before I give Prince a gold star, let me set up the shit. Let me go back to an evening when Prince and I took in a movie. We went to see *The Idolmaker*, a biopic based on Bob Marcucci, the dude who discovered Frankie Avalon and Fabian. The situation was a little like Colonel Parker and Elvis. As we watched the story of a manager manipulating the world around him, I could hear Prince thinking. He saw himself as an idolmaker.

In that mode, Prince finally made good on his promise to get me a deal. And when Prince moved, he moved fast. It all happened in a flash.

His vision remained a band, not a male solo artist. I think he saw a male solo artist as competition he didn't need.

*Wrong. Competition never bothered me. Never frightened me. Competition only motivated me 2 reach higher. U remember what I did at the 2004 Rock & Roll Hall of Fame jam with Jeff Lynne & Tom Petty. U remember my solo on "As My Guitar Gently Weeps"?*

Sure. Who doesn't remember that? You rose to the competitive occasion. But it's one thing to compete with your peers and another to create competition from your own camp. In my view, the idea was to develop musical units that would augment the main star—you—and not compete with you. That's why a band made sense.

Always in a hurry, you engaged me to put out a "band" record before I put together a band. And, true to form, you'd be the principal producer of that record. That was okay with me. I was thrilled to be your cowriter and coproducer. "Party Up" had shown you I could hold my own in the studio.

I already mentioned a couple of times when you used me as a drummer on your songs. Didn't get the credit and didn't care. It was enough to know that my grooves were working for you. You also had me fooling with the keyboard and guitar. You saw that I could do what you could do—essentially go from instrument to instrument—and you encouraged that . . . to an extent.

*Encouraged it more than anyone else in your life.*

Yes, and the encouragement got me doing things I never knew I could do. The story of making the first album, the one that would be known as *The Time*, is especially strange since the band that came to be known as The Time never played on the record.

It was just me and Prince at his Kiowa Trail home studio in Chanhassen, southwest of Minneapolis. Prince dug the anonymity of the burbs. We did the whole record in a flash, together turning out six songs. But there was more to it than just our time in the studio.

We'd go out to clubs together to see what was drawing dancers to the dance floor. The Brothers Johnson's "Stomp." Shalamar's "The Second Time Around." Nile Rodgers and Bernard Edwards getting Diana Ross to declare, "I'm Coming Out." Man, we studied those hits like mad scientists. We studied the rhythm tracks, the horn punches, the synth effects, the background vocals—the whole freakin' package. I'm not saying we stole anything. Prince had ideas of his own, and in my own way, so did I. But before we got down to work, we wanted to see exactly what was working in the clubs.

Part of the great pleasure of being in Prince's company was being absorbed by his obsession with music. His knowledge was vast. Our tastes overlapped in some areas but there were differences. I was higher on the fusion bands than Prince. I turned him on to Mahavishnu Orchestra. Because I was more a drummer and he more a guitarist, I was able to get him to listen to the astounding work of David Garibaldi of Tower of Power. Prince appreciated percussive subtlety.

Prince was crazy for Miles Davis. I dug Miles from *Kind of Blue* and *Bitches Brew*. I also followed Miles when he later hooked up with producer Tommy LiPuma and master bassist Marcus Miller and turned out *Tutu*. But Prince knew Miles's stuff from the '50s. Maybe because Prince's dad was a jazz musician or maybe because Prince could wrap his mind around bebop, he talked about Miles's records on the Prestige and Blue labels. He talked about how Miles had recruited the greatest virtuosos of his time—John Coltrane, Cannonball Adderley, Herbie Hancock, Tony Williams, Wayne Shorter, Keith Jarrett—but it was more than music that drew Prince to Miles. It was Miles's attitude. Miles's swagger. Miles's chameleonlike ability to adapt to musical fashions while inventing new fashions of his own.

Prince would talk about how Miles and Miles alone could get away with turning his back to the audience. He did it as a way of saying, "You don't matter as much as the music." Prince also dug that Miles broke the mold when it came to dress. Jazz musicians, like Prince's dad, were hardly into clothes. They were mostly conservative dressers. But as time went on, Miles strutted onto the stage like a rock star, wearing far-out metallic designs by avant-garde designers like Issey Miyake.

Prince had a thing for Joni Mitchell. He had all her records, knew all her songs, dug her voice, her writing, and especially her lyrics. I didn't feel Joni the way Prince did, but I did agree with him about Bob Dylan. We both saw Dylan as a towering songwriter. Prince was especially impressed with the depth of his catalog. A wildly prolific writer himself, Prince looked to Dylan as a model of productivity. He also dug the great range of Dylan's subject matter, not to mention his blues roots. For my part, I appreciated the strength of his songs—"Blowin' in the Wind," "Maggie's Farm," "Like a Rolling Stone"—but the gruffness of his voice left me a little cold.

There were nights when Prince and I did nothing but sit around and listen to the Beatles. He talked about *Sgt. Pepper's Lonely Hearts Club Band* as a revolutionary record. He loved how the Beatles, like Miles, were able to reinvent themselves. He knew that in pop culture, where tastes shift like the wind, reinvention is the key to sustaining success.

I turned Prince on to Frank Zappa. I'd practically worn out my copy of *Apostrophe* with that suite of songs, "Don't Eat the Yellow Snow." Prince immediately heard what I heard: musicality on the highest level, imagination let loose, balls-out humor, and originality that inspired us both.

So when it was time for Prince and me to go to his Kiowa Trail home studio and get serious about cutting tracks, our heads were filled with influences. Yet, like Zappa, our purpose was to be shockingly original while cranking grooves that even flat-footed wallflowers couldn't resist.

We focused like lasers and caught lightning in a bottle. To mess up my metaphors even more, I'd have to call it a deep dive into our feeling for funk. There were six songs that blended together like a musical mosaic. Listening to it, it's hard to say where Prince stops and I begin.

For the most part, I worked up the tracks. But Prince definitely added flavors. Instrumentally, Prince was on guitar and bass and I was on drums. Matt Fink added synth lines and Prince brought in some ladies for backgrounds, but I sang lead on all the songs. I'm not sure I'd ever have found the wherewithal to do that were it not for Prince.

But certain people—and Prince was one of them—don't believe in limitations. They blow right past them.

"You got your own personality," he'd say. "Your own sound. Just express it. Don't need to be afraid of nothing. You got the goods."

Coming from my mentor, that meant the world to me.

Prince saw that as a singer, I could be coy and even sexy. That was a little strange because coyness and sexiness had never been big parts of my real personality. But a new reality was emerging. A new me. With Prince egging me on, it felt great. Never thought of myself as distinctive before. Had always thought of myself as a drummer. But this was different. This was good. And of course being alone in a studio with Prince, turning out fresh funk day after day, was both a blast and an education.

The record was in the can, and if we'd been honest we should have called it *Prince Introduces Morris*. But Prince saw this as the debut album of a band that would be part of his ever-growing musical franchise. Given how Prince could run hot and cold on stuff, I wasn't completely convinced the record would ever come out. After it was complete, he turned his attention away from me and fell deep into other projects with other musicians. Naturally that made me crazy, but being driven crazy is the price you paid for being around Prince.

A few weeks went by. I went back to taking whatever drumming gigs I could get. I was playing a club called PJ Clark's in St. Paul when someone called me to the phone.

*Let me tell this story, bro.*

Go ahead.

*I said, "Morris, what u doing?" U said, "Making $35 a night banging the drums." I said, "U better quit that nonsense*

*& hurry up & put your band 2gether." U said, "What's the hurry?" I said, "U got a hit. 'Get It Up' dropped & it's a hit.' Now u really need a band. U also need a name. But I got that covered."*

Prince was listening to the Fixx, some cats from London, and thought a name like the Nerve might capture that New Wave culture. I didn't mind the Nerve, but when he said The Time, I blurted out, "That's hip. That's it. 'The Time' says it all."

It said we were current, we were on time or maybe even ahead of time. It said we had time. We were time. Time never grows old. And you never run out of time. Time's endless. Time's constant. Time's with us every ticktock of the clock. Time's always on our mind. Time keeps us going. Time's always moving ahead. Prince had set us in motion, and for years we'd be racing one hundred miles per hour.

So we had a name. Now we needed a band. I didn't need to look around for long. I knew the local scene upside down. The same band that had been competing with Grand Central back in high school towered above all others. Talkin' 'bout Flyte Time.

Prince was hesitant. Maybe he thought Flyte Time was too good. They'd always been self-sufficient. Like Prince, they might have possessed a touch of arrogance about their unsurpassed chops. Because I was also candid with Prince, I didn't hesitate to ask him whether he felt threatened. He denied it, so I pushed my argument. "The only criterion," I said, "is to pick the best players out there. Nothing else matters."

The plain fact was that Jimmy Jam and Terry Lewis's band was slammin' harder than ever. I didn't think I needed the horns because the template Prince and I had created on the first yet-to-be-released Time album was hornless. But I needed the core of the band. That was Jimmy on keys, Terry on bass, Jellybean Johnson on drums, Monte Moir on synth, and vocalist Alexander O'Neal. Can't say enough about these cats.

Let's start out with Jimmy. Jimmy was always a good guy, but back in the day he could be a little headstrong. Later in life he chilled until we became close as brothers. Despite his attitude, I knew that while no one was Prince, Jimmy belonged in the genius category. He had crazy chops. His best friend, Terry Lewis, was a fantastic bass player. Jellybean was the greatest straight-up funk drummer since the glory days of James Brown, Monte both a smooth blue-eyed soul singer and a bad man on synth, and Alexander a heavyweight champ in the Otis Redding–Teddy Pendergrass–Charlie Wilson tradition. All five supertalented. We were missing only one element: a firebrand guitarist.

A buddy from the Enterprise Band of Pleasure mentioned someone from Rock Island, Illinois. "This motherfucker will scare you," he said. "He's so bad he'll scare Prince." Hearing is believing, and as soon as I heard a cassette of Jesse Johnson's twenty-minute guitar solos, I was a believer. When I played the tape for Prince, he raised an eyebrow. That's all I needed to see. Prince simply nodded and said, "Get him."

I got Jesse to Minneapolis, where he slept on my couch till he found a place of his own. No question, Jesse was a skyrocketing guitar virtuoso cut out of the same Jimi Hendrix–Jeff Beck–Jimmy Page–Carlos Santana cloth as Prince. Like Prince, he was a Gemini. Outgoing and withdrawn, funny and serious, focused and restless—all at once.

Jimmy, Terry, Monte, and Jellybean were good to go. They saw the same thing the whole world was seeing: Prince was red-hot. Like every other musician in Minneapolis, they wanted in. Good as they were, they hadn't broken through to national fame. Prince had. He was that much better than the rest of us—more driven, cagier about his look, ballsier about putting sex in the middle of the mix. So they were more than ready to drop Flyte Time and join Team Prince. Jesse Johnson felt the same. The only holdout was Alexander O'Neal.

That pained me because Alexander was flat-out great. He could put The Time on his broad shoulders and carry us all the way up the charts. Even though I'd sung lead vocals on the record, he had to be our lead vocalist.

"Not enough paper" was all he said. "I need more."

I understood. Prince was paying minimum money. It was all on the come. But the upside was huge. It had to be worth the risk. Alexander, though, didn't see it that way. He saw it as exploitation. There was something to admire about his hard-nosed attitude. He'd been around the block. We all had. Musicians get fucked. We get cheated out of songwriter credits; we give away our production ideas; we never see royalties. The tradition of cheating musicians—especially black musicians—goes back a hundred years. Sidemen especially have suffered a miserable fate. So I couldn't really argue with Alexander. All I could say was that I was sorry.

*Turned out good 4 u, though, didn't it?*

You might say that. Without Alexander singing lead, Prince made it clear I'd be the singer. That both excited and scared me. Excited because by coproducing The Time album with Prince, I'd learned I could turn out lead vocals. But scared because when it came to no-nonsense soul singing, I did not put myself in the same category as Alexander O'Neal.

But before Prince chimes in again, let me co-opt him by saying that yes, he was the cat who turned me into a singer. He was the one who said that this band could express my personality, just as the Revolution would express Prince's musical vision. The problem had to do with something I hadn't heard of then: ego-merging.

Prince saw me as an extension of himself. I was his creation. That was okay with me since, as a creator, Prince was masterful. He presumed I'd always go along with his weird emotional dynamic. And for a long time I did. I'd have been a fool not to. Prince had already gotten over, and now he was trying to get me over. Why fight that? I didn't. Only later would I learn that ego-merging is a messy business unless one of the egos is prepared to be swallowed up by the other. But that's getting ahead of the story.

When this record was ready to be released, I wasn't thinking about anything except success.

I was sold.

The band was formed.

The big irony was that we did a cover photograph for the debut album, *The Time*, on which these musicians had not played. No matter; there we were—Jimmy, Terry, Monte, Jellybean, Jesse, and me standing in the center wearing white bucks and a slim white tie. The hype was heating up. The promo was rolling. Shit was jumping off faster than we could ever have imagined.

And then it got even faster.

# 9

# THE ELECTRIFYING MOJO

When The Time's first album came out, the credits read, "Produced by Morris Day & Jamie Starr." Naturally Prince was Jamie. He used a pseudonym so as not to confuse his solo persona with his role of a behind-the-scenes producer.

*I was hardly confused.*

You ain't reading me right. I'm not saying you were confused. Saying the opposite. You knew exactly where to go and how to get there. It all started working. You were the man out front but also the man at the controls. It was all about control.

Prince had control over the entire operation: recording, producing, management. The Time was managed by the cats Prince had picked to do his bidding—Bob Cavallo, Joe Ruffalo, and Steve Fargnoli. They booked our first tour. Our first gig was a showcase for Warner Brothers. We went over big. So when we hit the road we were expecting something even bigger. But what we got was the chitlin circuit.

Welcome to Nowhere, Alabama.

On a lonely Thursday night, we were tooling around in our beat-up bus looking for the Starlight. We figured it had to be farther down the road, a major venue outside Montgomery. It couldn't be this Starlight barroom we spotted off the highway, where half the letters in the neon name were burned out. Couldn't be, but was.

We unloaded and went in. No dressing room. No crowd. Just two cats drinking at the bar. The owner assured us the crowd would be coming later. A big wall cut through the center of the tiny stage, meaning half the band would be playing to one side of the room and half the band to the other. We went back out to the minivan to change. Went back inside to tune up. Still no crowd. At nine o'clock we kicked off our set. The "crowd" numbered no more than a dozen. When we played our hit single, "Get It Up," no one got up. No one danced. No one knew the jam. The applause was scattered. The folks were more interested in their drinks than our music.

The bus itself was nasty. Stank of gasoline. There was a messed-up VHS machine where a certain porn movie was in heavy rotation. I ain't gonna sermonize against porn, but this particular smut had elements of a horror film, and, man, do I hate horror films. Couldn't even look at the thing. So I demanded that we watch *The Flintstones* instead. One of the characters on the show was a prehistoric bird called Pterodactyl. During one episode Fred Flintstone and his crew actually do a Pterodactyl dance where they flap their wings. Pterodactyl flew into our lives a little bit later. Stand by for the explanation.

We made our way through the South. Little by little, enthusiasm began to build, but the enthusiasm did not spill over. It stayed mild. In some cities our single was being played and the party people got to dancing. As the lead man, I was working hard to make it look easy, carefully crafting my stage chatter, my iceberg-cool attitude.

But it wasn't till we got to Motown that good vibes were set in motion. That's because the beloved deejay Charles Johnson, the man who calls himself the Electrifying Mojo, broke our record in Detroit. Mojo had done the same for the singles off Prince's first two albums. He loved him some Prince and, in turn, showered the same love on us.

When The Time hit the 20 Grand, the fabled club where '60s superstars like the Temptations and Supremes had headlined, our well-oiled musical machine had really started to hum. We knew Mojo had been hyping us hard but still weren't ready for the girls rushing the stage. My first thought was that management had arranged the rush—anything to build excitement around us. But the rush was real. The chicks really were trying to get to us. Which was a beautiful thing. Maybe too beautiful.

Emotionally, I'm not sure I was ready for all this love. Never really had known adulation before. Had to look the word up in the dictionary. To be adored was a new phenomenon, especially for a freckle-faced kid from the projects. Suddenly, though, that kid was cool, not simply Cool in the Corner but Cool in the Center. I was the center of attention. I was wearing a new Cool Cloak I had never worn before. I mean that literally. I'd always striven to be a sharp dresser, but suddenly I was beyond sharp. I was sparkling.

*U were tripping.*

You bet I was. I was tripping like an astronaut shot into space. Instead of me tentatively going after chicks, chicks were aggressively coming after me. Every red-blooded boy's dream come true. I lacked the wherewithal to resist. Didn't even try to resist. If it meant ruining my relationship with Jennifer, I was too weak—too young, too horny, too struck by my own stardom—to know better. I just wanted more of everything. More of the ladies, more of the highs, more of the prime weed, and increasingly more of the blow. This was the '80s. While Nancy Reagan was saying, "Just say no," I was saying, "Just say yes."

Yes to the long-legged honey in Chicago, yes to the fat joint stealthily slipped into my pocket by a fan in Oakland, yes to a line of pure Colombian lined up on a glass coffee table in a posh Hollywood hotel.

It was all working for me. And if that wasn't enough, I fell into the mirror routine. That routine is now approaching its fortieth anniversary as a permanent part of my stage presentation.

It all started during a rehearsal. Our first tour was over and we were gearing up for the second. Prince fell by to supervise. He was thinking of having us open for him and wanted us to sharpen our moves.

I was singing "Cool," the signature song off the first record, a production representing the perfect Prince/Morris collaboration. I say perfect because it was a reflection of Prince's feelings about himself projected onto me. Not that I didn't like the projection. I loved it.

The projection was that the singer was the coolest cat on the planet. He was rich beyond reason—had all the cars, diamonds, and houses money could buy. If Prince sang this song, it might make him seem arrogant and egotistical. But coming from the character he was creating—me—it worked. Yes, I was becoming a cool cat, but at the same time I was a parody of a cool cat. I was comically cool. I was so cool that you could laugh at my coolness. So cool, in fact, that the only way to express my coolness was through a long vocal chant over the extended instrumental vamp: "Ain't nobody bad like me." The song has me falling in love with my coolness, falling in love with myself. Later someone told me that's the story of Narcissus, who, looking in the pool, falls in love with his own reflection. No doubt Prince was a narcissist.

*Wait a minute, then who r u?*

A narcissist also. But a narcissist trained by a master narcissist teaching me all the tricks of the trade.

*U r blaming me.*

I'm thanking your narcissistic ass for taking me on. How I followed through on your lessons is my business, my responsibility. I was happy to jump on your train and go along for the ride. In some ways, I'm still on that train. So I ain't blamin'. Just explainin'.

Explainin' how, for instance, one of my signature moves came into being. Happened at our rehearsal spot, a club that was empty during the days. Called YAASM (Young African American Society of Men), it was run by a heavy cat called Weaver. Weaver wouldn't stand for no bullshit. Cross him and he'd knock your ass down with a single punch. He let us use his place with the provision that we not fuck up two things: The first was his juice machine: "Don't ever touch it," he said. And the second was his tittie lamp: "Don't ever break it." He called it that 'cause the base of the lamp was shaped like a pair of luscious female breasts.

One day we were in there rehearsing with Prince. Prince loved to orchestrate these rehearsals. He'd work us hours longer than we'd want to. I was crooning the part of the song "Cool" where the singer is so in love with his good looks that he calls for a mirror. Well, as it turns out, YAASM had walls of ornate mirrors. Without being told to, Jerome Benton snatched a big ol' gold-framed mirror off the wall and brought it to me. Jerome, Terry Lewis's brother, had been working as our roadie. Now, with mirror in hand, he stood in front of me so I could lovingly admire myself. Gazing at my reflection, smoothing my hair, and straightening my tie, I became a funky ghetto-fabulous version of Narcissus. The entire scenario riveted Prince. He fell out laughing. Thought that was the funniest shit he'd ever seen. Loved it so much he said . . .

*"That's a keeper." I knew u had 2 put that in the act.*

Damn straight. We all knew it. It felt right. It added to the ever-evolving ever-cool Morris Day character. Morris needed to have his man on hand at all times. He needed a valet.

How could I not like it? I hadn't yet been told the end of the story of Narcissus, who, after falling in love with his own image, loses his mind and kills himself. All I knew was that Prince/Jamie Starr was masterfully shaping his own star. I didn't see the downside and neither did Prince/Jamie.

I understood that in the competitive world of pop music, you needed more than a funky beat. Sometimes you needed more than a sexy song. Sometimes you needed a gimmick. No doubt the mirror was a gimmick, but a good one.

The kiss-off to that story, though, is that when Jerome put the mirror back on the wall, he knocked into the tittie lamp and broke the thing. We tried gluing it, but all the king's horses and all the king's men couldn't put those big breasts back together again. Jesse Johnson also messed up the juicer. Weaver 'bout had a fit and promptly put us out. But Jerome "Mirror Man" Benton, a cat everyone loved, became our secret weapon.

The Time found its mojo. We were turning out hits. No surprise, then, that Prince rushed us into the studio for our second album. We began just as we had begun the first album—me and Prince alone. He remained the principal—principal writer, principal arranger, principal producer. I got credit on two of the songs—"777-9311" and "Gigolos Get Lonely Too," but in terms of composition, Prince was the pilot and I was his wingman. The recording sessions themselves were scattered. We started off in Prince's Minneapolis studio but he was always eager to run off to LA. Let it be known that Prince was never immune to the lure of Hollywood. (For that matter, me either.) There we cut at Sunset and Cherokee, two famous studios, where some of The Time members sang backgrounds or added musical flourishes. By then Prince had put together Vanity 6 and had the girls sing backgrounds on a long track we called "The Walk."

The key song on this second album was "Gigolos Get Lonely Too," a midtempo gem for which I received cocredit but, again, was born out of Prince's fertile imagination. It gave me a chance to go deep. In the old days, they might have called it a blues ballad because the cat singing the song has a case of the sure-enough blues. He's a playa who's played out. At various times that turned out to be the story of my life. The lyrics are sad while the groove is anything but. The groove is intoxicating and, like I'm still saying at my shows, if you can't feel it, brotha, you can't feel nothing.

*What Time Is It?* is a lighthearted record. Prince had the good sense to let us fool around and do some of our silly verbal routines. On "OneDayI'mGonnaBeSomebody," for instance, me and the boys started chanting "We don't like New Wave!" even though we knew Prince did. Prince could have edited out the chant, but he let it stay.

He thought it was funny. He understood that The Time was rooted in whimsy.

Prince came up with the album title, *What Time Is It?* And wanted me and me alone on the cover. So there I am checking my gold wristwatch against a background of assorted clocks on the wall behind me. I'm wearing a fancy brocade blazer and have a befuddled look on my face. If I look surprised, well, I was surprised at the sudden pace of our success. If I look clownish, well, the record certainly contained clownish scenarios of me flirting with foxy ladies.

The inside cover featured smaller black-and-white photos of the other cats—Terry, Jimmy, Jesse, Jellybean, and Monte. My inside photo was not me; instead it showed a pair of fancy black-and-white spats underscored with the caption "Stacy Adams."

We were steppin'. The record had three hit singles. Stayed on the charts for months. Next thing we knew Prince had us open for him on the worldwide tour he was planning to promote his fourth album, *Controversy*. To put things in perspective, *What Time Is It?* went gold while *Controversy* went platinum.

You might think all this good fortune would make us one big happy family. Think again.

# 10

# EGG ON YOUR FACE

Prince ain't gonna like what I'm about to write.

*Try me.*

You felt threatened by how good The Time became.

*If I was threatened, y would I have u open 4 me?*

The Time was definitely your creation, but until you heard us live night after night, you didn't realize how good we were. You'd created a monster that suddenly had a chance of being bigger than you.

*Not buying it. Makes no sense. 'Cause if that were the case, I'd never have put u & The Time in the movies.*

You keep jumping ahead. We'll get to that later.

*Deal with it now. U don't wanna deal with it 'cause it blows up your case.*

Hey, man, it only strengthens my case. But right now I ain't making no case. Just making an observation. Just trying to keep this story moving.

The *Controversy* album, Prince's fourth in three years, included some political songs and a few anti-Reagan riffs, but the big hit was "Do Me, Baby," a straight-out sex plea. Word is that the song was really written by André Cymone, not Prince. I don't know for sure. All I do know is that André, one of the world's great guys, had a falling-out with Prince. That took me by surprise. It was Prince and André who had started together in Grand Central. Like me, André was one of Prince's closest collaborators. Plus André was an easygoing cat. I didn't get in the middle of it. Bottom line was that by the start of the Controversy Tour, André was no longer playing bass in Prince's band. André would go on to make great albums of his own—plus huge hits with former Shalamar singer Jody Watley, who was then his wife. Staying cool with Prince, no matter how far you went back with him, wasn't easy.

*Any easier than staying cool with cats making claims on songs I'd written? I've written so many songs that it's easy 4 someone 2 come around & say, "Oh, yeah, that's my melody" or "Oh, yeah, that's my hook."*

I don't know how it went down between you and André. Don't know how many of André's bass lines wound up as essential components to your compositions.

Prince worked off competition. Me too. I whipped up The Time the best I could. Opening for Prince, I wanted to scare him. Wanted him to hear that we weren't just funky but so goddamn funky he'd have to think twice about how to outfunk us. I can't apologize for this attitude because it's an attitude I learned from him. Before Prince, my work ethic was decent but hardly ferocious. Prince taught me ferocity. Before Prince, my competitive spirit was there but inactive. Prince activated it.

It all came together on the Controversy Tour, which started in Pittsburgh and ended up in Cincinnati four months later in mid-

March 1982. By then I had traded in the '79 Mustang Prince had bought me for a brand-spanking-new Mustang paid for with my own cash. The Time really came into our own. We were in take-no-prisoners mode. Prince liked it and he didn't. He liked the fact that his creation was smokin' hot but didn't like the pressure of having to follow us. His band felt the same way. Audiences have only so much energy. And if the opening act is so explosive that much of their energy is drained, the headliners ain't gonna be real happy.

*The headliner was doing just fine.*

The headliner was drawing big crowds and great reviews. Without the headliner, the opening act would be playing to an empty arena. But those big crowds and great reviews were also embracing The Time. We were developing a fan base independent of the headliner.

All this contributed to growing tension. Over these four months, our show was getting slicker every night. Jerome not only was bringing out the mirror to let me bathe in my cool reflection, but also added percussive muscle to Jellybean's beefed-up beats.

During the tour itself, there was little contact with Prince. On the road, he liked to do what he often did at home: make himself scarce. You didn't just fall by his dressing room to pay an unannounced visit. His door remained closed. Because we were so close, we could feel each other's vibes from afar. I knew he was seething about The Time getting so much sugar from the fans. And I knew that by pushing my band as hard as I could, I was intent on getting even more sugar.

There was even competition when it came to partying. Let's say Prince and his crew were on floor 20 and we were down on floor 10. Well, the floor 10 party—The Time party—was a get-down ghetto party. Might have been on floor 10, but, baby, we turned floor 10 into the basement, complete with half-clad or unclad bodies doing the boogaloo with lampshades on their heads. Party in the hallway. Party in the hospitality suite. Party in the bedrooms. Drinking. Smoking. Coking. Couples moaning and boning without caring who be watching.

Meanwhile, the floor 20 parties were strictly suburban. Uptight. Butlers and dry martinis. A pianist playing quiet cocktail jazz. Gentlemen in tuxes whispering in the corner. Sophisticated ladies.

At one point Prince got bored with his parties. I know that 'cause, hearing how we were having a blast, he showed up on floor 10. He had to see what was happenin'. Prince made his entrance on the back of his bodyguard, Big Chick, real name Charles Huntsberry, a mountain of a man and a sweetheart of a guy. Big Chick gave Prince a feeling of big security. But when Prince made his grand entrance and none of the party people acknowledged his grandeur—no one gave a shit that he was there—Prince got pissed and left. More bad feeling. The competition between the warring camps got fierce.

By the time the last gig came around in Cincinnati, the dam broke. We were in the middle of our set, jamming hard on "Cool," when just as Jerome was putting up the mirror for me to admire myself, rotten eggs started flying in our direction. I looked over at the wings and saw that the assailants were members of Prince's band. A couple of the eggs splattered on my cats. Before we had time to clean up the yolk, Prince's assholes were throwing rotten garbage at us. Somehow we finished the set, but the audience was bewildered. They couldn't get their groove on because our groove had been undermined by what amounted to a high school food fight.

Truth is, we were ready to fight back. But our counteroffensive was hampered when Prince's boys handcuffed Jesse Johnson to a coat rack welded to the wall. By the time we sprung him loose, Prince's act was over. Back at the hotel, though, my boys were ready to rock and suddenly the shit got violent. No broken bones but punches thrown and a couple of hotel rooms wrecked.

When the battle died down, I banged on Prince's door. He let me in and our verbal fight was on. He was worried about the damage we'd done to the hotel. I was screaming that he'd started the rout by putting his cats up to it. He denied that.

*Still do. Musicians r always pulling pranks. Was out of my control.*

Bullshit, brother. Everyone knew nothing was out of your control. You also knew that it took a lot to upset me. I'd never had this kind of confrontation with you before. But this shit was serious. Your dudes had fucked up our set. Why?

Your only answer was I'd have to pay the cost of the ruined hotel rooms. I said, "Fuck that shit." But I wound up paying it anyway.

That might have done it. That night might have fractured our friendship right there and then. But in Prince's world, things moved so quickly that even vicious fights could be forgotten in a flash. Especially when another whirlwind tour was coming. He still wanted The Time as his opening act. We still wanted to ride his rocket ship to the moon. He promised us a raise—maybe as a way to make up for the egg fight—and even though the raise wasn't much, he did lay out four months' worth of steady work, four months when The Time could reach bigger crowds from one end of the country to another.

This was the winter of 1982, after he'd dropped *1999*, his fifth and by far most successful album to date. The title track and "Little Red Corvette" turned into monster hits. For the first time, *1999* placed Prince on the top of the charts, not just in the United States but all over the world. This shit was mega and I'd be a fool not to be part of it.

But Prince being Prince didn't just drop a new album of his own. He'd been developing still another group: Vanity 6. The origin of that act goes back a few years to another time Prince and I watched a movie together. We were at his crib in Chanhassen, where he had a VHS copy of *A Star Is Born*, the Barbra Streisand/Kris Kristofferson version from '76. He was fascinated by the idea of a male rock star turning an unknown female singer into a star herself. Combine that with all that time he spent watching the Mary Jane Girls open up for Rick James.

In 1980 Denise Matthews was Rick's date at the American Music Awards. She was a knockout. That night Prince managed to strike up a conversation with her. A little later she turned up in Minneapolis by Prince's side. I don't know all the ins and outs except to say that this was the same period when Prince was planning a three-lady vocal group he wanted to call the Hookers. (Maybe he got the idea from Bette Midler's Harlettes.) He talked about naming the lead singer Vagina. Not too subtle, but when it came to sex, Prince's strong card was not subtlety. He dropped those names but followed through on the idea of a trio. Denise became Vanity. Don't ask me why Prince called the group Vanity 6 instead of Vanity 3.

*Mystery. Real mysteries remain unsolved. Solve a mystery & it's no longer a mystery.*

Also wasn't no mystery why the second single off *Vanity 6*, "Nasty Girl," was a smash, another Prince invention that hit the airwaves right on time. Rick James claimed that the whole sexy setup came from him, but hell, Ray Charles had the Raelettes and Ike Turner had the Ikettes way back when. Was hardly nothing new. What was new was Prince's input. His terminology—the very word *nasty*—sparked the flame. Cats have been dreaming about bedding a nasty girl since Samson and Delilah. Prince molded Vanity in his signature seductive mode. Didn't hurt that he cranked out an especially nasty groove that worked in both the ballroom and the bedroom. Folks be dancing as well as boning to Prince's latest ditty.

So Prince had Vanity 6 open his 1999/Triple Threat Tour. He put them in alluring getups and used The Time as their backup band. We were happy to oblige but not all that happy when he insisted that we play behind a closed curtain while the girls were out front. He wanted the gorgeous gals to command the audience without distraction. For our trouble we got an extra $250.

*U gotta admit it made sense.*

To you, not to us. We felt we were being hidden. You dug it 'cause it was good for the flow of the show. When Vanity 6 had sung their five-song set, the curtains parted and right then and there The Time could start throwing down.

Throughout the long 1999 Tour, we kept sharpening our musical knives. We were cutting it up big time. Of the triple threats—Vanity

6, The Time, and the boss himself—we wanted to be the most threatening. We hadn't forgotten that fight in Cincy. Our way of getting back was to drive the audience wild. Wipe them out before Prince came on after intermission.

*Didn't work out that way.*

I'll give that to you. You drove 'em even crazier, but in the meantime our cred as a premier funk band was building. I got an offer, for example, to produce Evelyn "Champagne" King, who'd been riding high with her "Shame" and "Love Come Down." She needed a follow-up hit and offered me $75,000 to produce her. I asked your permission. I'd do it after the tour was over and wouldn't miss a single date. No skin off your back. Figured you wouldn't mind.

Figured wrong. You were adamant. No outside gigs. We worked for you and you alone. I started to argue, but why? I knew I couldn't win. All I knew was to stay on my grind.

Then came the day that, in Prince lore, has lived in infamy. Jimmy Jam and Terry Lewis missed a gig. We'd played New York's Radio City on Monday, March 21, 1983. Our next date wasn't till Thursday in San Antonio. Jimmy and Terry used that time to fly to Georgia, where, without Prince's knowledge, they were producing the SOS Band. While they were in the studio, an unexpected snowstorm shut down the Atlanta airport. Jimmy and Terry couldn't get to Texas in time to make our gig. Jerome had to pretend to be playing the bass while Prince, behind the curtain, was actually plucking the notes.

Prince was furious. He called me to the dressing room and said, "Fire Jimmy and Terry." I didn't want to. I refused to fire them. Since childhood, I loved when original members stayed together. Broke my heart when Lenny Williams left Tower of Power. Hated it when Lionel Richie split from the Commodores. Couldn't stand it when David Lee Roth ran out of Van Halen. I wanted my band intact. Wasn't no replacing Jimmy and Terry. They were the best. As the Flyte Time leaders, they'd given up a lot to get behind The Time. Didn't matter that they missed one gig. We weren't paid a fortune for the 1999 Tour anyway, and it was understandable that they were looking to earn extra bread as outside producers. I understood. I wanted to do the same. Last thing I wanted to do was fire them.

*U read what I told* Rolling Stone *magazine about that?*

I read where you made up some shit, saying the decision was mine. It wasn't. You gonna claim that you didn't run the whole show?

*Turned out 2 b the best thing that could have happened 2 Jam & Lewis.*

Sure, but at the time you didn't know that. You didn't foresee Jimmy and Terry going on to produce Janet Jackson. All you saw was them walking out the door. You were the one who pulled the trigger, not me. I hated that. Hated it because I not only loved Jimmy and Terry but you were ripping out the very heart of the band. And, in the process, breaking my heart.

*Let's not get melodramatic.*

It *was* big drama. Maybe not for you. But for me. It also made me realize that while I was band leader, the band didn't belong to me. It belonged to you. And though I recognized you as a crazy-ass genius, I also saw you putting your feelings above everyone else's.

The departure of Jimmy and Terry was a huge blow. At the time, I was probably pissed at myself for not telling you to go fuck yourself and quitting your whole operation. I didn't do that because the crazy-ass genius part of you was still a lure. I wanted to be associated with that genius.

I know I'm talented, but I'm no genius. Even having been around your genius for all those years, it's hard to put myself in your head. A genius can be overwhelmed by the creative currency shooting through his brain. That can not only put him on edge but make him a little nuts. I guess one way the genius copes with dealing with all that pounding energy is to try to control the world around him. Maybe the genius feels like if he can't control that energy, he'll blow up.

Prince, of course, did blow up. In 1983 the only artist who had blown up bigger than him was Michael Jackson on the heels of *Thriller*. Michael's supersonic success only pushed Prince to come up with what he thought would be an even bigger supersonic success. Firing Jimmy Jam and Terry Lewis and breaking up The Time's original lineup was just a blip on his radar. He had a grand scheme in mind. Something none of us could ever imagine. Something so big—so different, so bold and daring—that it changed the game for all of us.

# 11

# PURPLE RAIN

When Prince fired Jimmy and Terry, I could have walked away. I could have reached out to them and said, "Fuck Prince. Stay in The Time. It's our band. We've got our own hits. We'll tour without him." I didn't do that. Why?

First of all, I was getting high—and being high hardly helps clarity. But no matter how high I might have been, I knew that trying to walk off with The Time would involve a legal entanglement I couldn't afford. By then Prince had major money. My minor money couldn't afford fancy lawyers. But it was more than my financial inability to walk away from the Prince machine. It was the plain fact that I didn't want to. I was part of Prince's magical enterprise just when the magic was spreading. He was going to make a movie. And not only that, he was making the damn movie in the dead of winter in Minneapolis.

Crazy? You bet. But did I want in? Hell, yes. Who doesn't wanna be in a movie? It's the ultimate show-biz fantasy. All my anger at Prince, all my frustrations at his controlling nature melted away once I heard the word *movie*. Movies are fun. Movies are seen by millions of fans. And besides, I didn't even have to go to Hollywood to make the movie. Hollywood was coming to Minneapolis. That's how much power Prince exerted.

For all this excitement, the process itself came close to falling apart. Fact is, I was hired, then fired, only to be hired again. Chaos is always hard to break down and *Purple Rain* was born, bred, and shot in chaos. Chaos resulted in triumph, but the triumph resulted in more chaos.

Prince dug the movies as well as movie stars. He always said that the biggest musical artists—going back to Judy Garland, Frank Sinatra, Elvis Presley, and Barbra Streisand—also became movie stars. Given his good looks, natural swag, and coy charm, he saw no reason why he couldn't become a movie star. And of course he was right. So I wasn't surprised that as soon as his music career hit the stratosphere, he wanted to make a splash on the silver screen. Couple that with the fact that MJ, Prince's chief competitor, was putting out a long video version of "Thriller" and had big film ambitions of his own. Prince wasn't about to be left behind. Fact is, Prince was determined to leap ahead. Let MJ make his long-form video. Prince would best him by making—and starring in—an actual wide-release feature film.

Hanging out with Prince, I heard how hard it was to get the film financed. The record industry saw Prince as a superstar, but Hollywood was skeptical. Even supersmart moguls like David Geffen couldn't see this movie making money. But telling Prince he couldn't do something was a guarantee that he'd do it. He used a lot of his own money to underwrite the $7 million budget and finally found a director. It happened because one of the guys he wanted, James Foley, who'd just directed Daryl Hannah in *Reckless*, said no. But the editor of that same film, Albert Magnoli, who'd never directed before, said yes.

Back during the 1999 Tour, Prince was talking about this movie. He had an idea for a story. The story, like so many of Prince's songs, was autobiographical. I heard it in bits and pieces. It was about a musician with two challenges—his career and his love life. His career isn't as big as he wants it to be, and he hasn't yet found the girl of his dreams. Combine that with the problems he's having with his parents—especially his dad—and you have the bare bones of the story.

That story didn't change much. When he brought in Magnoli and William Blinn, another writer, the story got a little darker, then a little lighter. The story was always evolving to the point where we, the characters Prince had chosen, never knew what was going on. Movies are shot in short segments, so without being shown the big picture, it's easy to feel lost. We were never shown the big picture until the actual premiere.

We were the supporting players. To keep the autobiographical edge, Prince was adamant in including me and The Time. He cast us in the role of his competition. Given how hard we had pushed him with our blistering opening set during the recent tours, that was close to Prince's reality. He also cast members of his own Revolution band, Wendy and Lisa, as frustrated side musicians trying to get the boss to hear their own songs. Also close to reality. The third element was Vanity 6. Because he and Vanity had parted ways, he found a substitute, a former beauty queen, LA Raiders cheerleader and TV actress Apollonia, another total knockout. To further increase the competitive heat, Prince set up a rivalry between me and him not only for musical superiority but for Apollonia. No doubt he'd come out winning on all fronts.

*U make it sound like u didn't benefit.*

I benefited big time. I not only accepted the role of the losing villain, I got into it. I dug it. Turned out to be fun. And also mind-bending. I say mind-bending because no one knew anything. The film went down in the weirdest way possible. Even though it was lights, camera, action, we were kept in the dark.

There was no big meeting—or for that matter, no meeting at all—where Prince called us together to explain the Big Concept. It was only him saying, "Hey, we're making a movie. Wanna be in it?" Well, of course I wanted to be in it. I also wanted to be paid. "I'll give you fifty grand," he said, "but that'll also cover your band." What he meant was that when we weren't on tour, The Time was on retainer. And that retainer was paid by me. I should've had a lawyer negotiate for me, but I knew Prince wouldn't put up with no lawyer. I didn't want to risk losing the chance to hit the big screen, and besides, as I said before, weed and blow weren't exactly helping me think straight.

My participation in the project nearly ended before it really got started. That's because we were given an acting coach, a dude I didn't like. He had these exercises. Pretend you're a weeping willow tree. Pretend you're a butterfly lost in the forest. Well, I didn't wanna be no weeping willow. I didn't wanna be no butterfly lost in the forest. I thought that was some dumb shit and said so. I turned into the class clown. So much so that word got back to Prince, who took me aside for a scolding. He said this was serious business and I better not fuck up or I'd be out on my ass. I'd be out of the movie. I'd be out of The Time. He'd banish me from his empire.

I heard him and I didn't. I heeded his warning and I didn't. I tried a little bit harder in class, but I still cut up. I still turned it into a joke. Something told me that yes, I probably did have some acting chops, but this class wasn't building them up. My acting chops were more of a natural thing. Like humor. Humor comes naturally to me.

The one cat who saw this was the director, Albert Magnoli. He came to a couple of those classes when I was acting the fool and suddenly saw the potential of my on-screen character. He had Prince back off. He started holding special sessions with me where he'd ask me to read the script out loud.

Albert was extra cool when he said, "If these words don't come natural to you, switch 'em up. Change the language any way you want. We want you to sound real."

That was a great request, and I did it. I rewrote a whole lot of my part. Looking back, though, the predicament was this: What was real?

Was I really cool, or was I pretending to be cool? When the cameras started to roll, the very thing I had been criticized for—cutting up—was the same thing that Magnoli and Prince were now praising me for. Without trying, I'd turned it all around. Now Magnoli and Prince saw me turning into a comic character that could give this dark movie the light side it needed.

All this was:

Confusing.

Exciting.

Difficult.

Easy.

Fun.

And not so much fun.

*Wasn't much fun 4 us when u wouldn't show up on set on time. I'd have 2 send out a patrol looking 4 u.*

No one wants to be on set at 5 a.m. Five a.m. ain't when I get up. Five a.m. is when I go to sleep.

*U were wasted half the time. U didn't take the thing seriously.*

And that's just why the thing worked. I took out the serious and put in the fun. The fun part was running around a movie set where dozens of women were running around in flimsy camisoles. We shot a lot of the scenes at First Avenue, a downtown Minneapolis club that had once been a Greyhound bus station. Its first name as a music venue was the Depot. Back in the day, groups like the Ramones, U2, and Iggy and the Stooges played there. When our homegrown bands came along—I'm talkin' 'bout Grand Central and Flyte Time—First Avenue wouldn't look at us twice. White bands for white fans were always preferred. Prince changed all that. His thing was to write something, arrange something, and then test it live. He saw First Avenue as a great testing ground. He liked the tight feeling of a place holding hundreds of people squeezed together, all eager to get grooved up. He liked that up-in-your face energy. He used First Avenue as his lab. Given his stature, he could have picked any place. He landed on First Avenue because it was right there in the heart of downtown Minneapolis. He transformed the club and single-handedly turned it into the hub of Minneapolis funk.

During the filming of *Purple Rain*, we were standing in front of First Avenue in the freezing cold. Makeup trailers were parked in the alleys. Generators broke down; heaters were always on the brink. But the show went on. The half-clad honeys waiting patiently until they were called into the club. Extras everywhere. My brother, Jesse, was an extra. Seemed like half of Minneapolis were extras.

Between rehearsals, sound checks, and the actual shooting, I felt chaos lurking around the corner. That wasn't fun. Impending doom is never fun. We had a first-time director, first-time star, first-time cast, first-time everything. Yet despite all the inexperience and out-of-breath last-minute preparations, despite the concern that it could really all collapse, it didn't. Cameras kept rolling. Scenes kept getting shot. Whether it'd all come together or not, who knew? Didn't matter. It was a force unto itself. The force was Prince.

Prince was on a natural high because he was pulling off the biggest operation of his life. I was on a drug high that I was somehow able to use to enhance my character. I'm not advocating drug use for singers or actors. That shit will kill you—and it damn near killed me. But I do have to report that in that dead of winter of 1983, I used my altered state to slip into a role that was both me and not me. The character I played bore my real name. I was "Morris." The character I played led my real band, The Time. The character I played had a love/hate relationship with the film's star, who had renamed himself the Kid. He did that to add to his mystique. And just as Morris was and was not Morris, the Kid was and was not the real Prince.

The real Prince did have a rough relationship with his parents, but not as rough as the one shown in the film. Prince's father and the Kid's father both played piano. Prince's father and the Kid's father both gave Prince a hard time. Prince did leave home, just as the Kid left home, to live in André Cymone's basement, the very basement re-created in the film.

Prince and I didn't have to re-create the competitive fire between us. It was boiling hot. Even when he saw that he needed my humor for the film to work, he stayed on my ass for being even a minute late. In one instance when I came on set behind schedule he was beside himself. He actually shoved me. I was about to lay him out when Jellybean grabbed me just as Big Chick grabbed Prince. The last thing this picture needed was two stars with black eyes. It was the only time we almost came to blows. I'm glad we didn't.

The drugs popping off in my brain might explain my behavior. But what explains Prince's fightin' behavior? He wasn't the violent type. What was going on? I have at least one explanation.

All during the making of the movie, Prince was in macho mode. I was there when he was booed at the Rolling Stones shows and called out for being effeminate, and I know that humiliation remained on his mind. Through the Kid, he retaliates. He answers those critics by dressing in black leather, zooming around town on a badass Harley, and seducing Apollonia, the foxiest chick since Pam Brown. He does this all with style and swag. In the midst of this manly action, he sings three of his greatest songs—"Let's Go Crazy," "When Doves Cry," and "Purple Rain." It's a triumph. But also overcompensation for his earlier image of sexual ambiguity.

*Man, what r u accusing me of?*

Not a fuckin' thing. When cats claimed you were gay, my response was always the same: "Try leaving him alone with your fine honey and see what happens." At the same time, you had your sense of sexual identity as mysterious and undefinable as your musical identity. Sexually, you gave the impression of being all over the place. Same with music: Don't even think about stuffing you in some category. Don't think about putting you in a box. And if anyone tried, you'd break out. You were always breaking out with some crazy new shit.

*Whatever u r doing, u r overanalyzing me 2 death.*

Ain't overanalyzing you enough. I truly believe Prince—or the Kid—is asking to be analyzed. Begging to be analyzed. That's what the mystique is all about. The mystique is saying, Think about me. Obsess on me. Dream of me. Try to figure me out.

*I never offered that invitation.*

Come on, bro. You cultivated it like crazy. Ain't sayin' it's bad. It worked like a motherfucker. You pulled it off. Film was huge. Soundtrack was huge. Fans went nuts.

*Let's get back 2 psychoanalyzing u.*

Cool. I willingly and even joyfully got sucked into your success. There's a Marvin Gaye line that talks 'bout getting drowned in a sea of happiness. That was me. As it became clearer that my role as your nemesis was becoming central to the film, I couldn't help but be happy. Interestingly enough, I didn't see that till the premiere. That was the first time I saw *Purple Rain* in its entirely. You never showed us the dailies. You never even showed us a rough cut. Far as I knew, most of my big scenes could have been dumped. But it went the other way. The spine of the story was the Kid's defeat—and humiliation—of Morris.

*But Morris & The Time got prime time in that film.*

And I'd be the last to say I didn't dig it. We played what turned out to be two of our biggest hits. Yes, Prince came up with the titles. If I suggested a title of my own, no matter how good, it was batted down. That stung. On the other hand, Prince's titles were so good the sting didn't last long.

"Jungle Love" was Prince's notion of uninhibited hot sex. The groove originated with Jesse Johnson's killer guitar line. I put my own hurting on it and the thing started sizzling like fresh meat on the grill. A tasty dish that still tastes good today.

"The Bird" was born out of a strange conflict. Onstage I'd come up with a move to a groove where I was flapping my arms. Prince got pissed. He thought I was mocking a dance move he made. I wasn't. I was actually modifying that dance move from the cartoon I mentioned earlier, *The Flintstones*. Prince said stop. I asked why. "You making me look bad," he insisted. I insisted he was paranoid so I kept on doing what I was doing. I realized I was doing a new kinda dance.

Now, coming up with a dance craze ain't exactly nothing new. Chubby Checker had his Twist. There was the Shimmy, the Swim, and the Locomotion. In one song alone—"Papa's Got a Brand New Bag"—James Brown gives a shout-out to the Jerk, the Fly, the Monkey, and the Mashed Potato. At some point, Prince did a boomerang. Yes, there were times when he reversed himself and changed up an attitude. Once Prince saw the audience eating up our stage moves he decided to name it rather than fight it. He called it the Bird, saying, "Morris, you win. Do this Bird to death. I think the thing's gonna fly."

The thing flew to number one.

Although the songs were huge, Prince made a point of *not* including them on the *Purple Rain* soundtrack, which wound up selling over twenty-five million copies. Because I'm a writer on both "Jungle Love" and "The Bird," if Prince had kept them on the soundtrack, I would have made a whole lot more than my $50,000 actor's fee. Given their importance in the film, there's no reason why they shouldn't have been on the soundtrack. It's hard to argue that other filler songs that made the soundtrack are better jams or more seminal to the story than the ones played by The Time. The world knows that when Prince sang "Let's Go Crazy" and "Purple Rain," he rose to a new level. But part of what spurred him on was the heat we provided with "Jungle Love" and "The Bird." Sure, he outdid us, but we also outdid ourselves. We deserved to be on that soundtrack.

*I had a dozen other songs I could have put on that soundtrack. Songs I'd written by myself. It was a Prince & the Revolution soundtrack, not a soundtrack of The Time.*

You got your bullshit arguments. I got mine. You had your power. I had none. You had the skill to scramble up elements of your life into a great movie. The way you incorporated those musical extensions of yourself—the Revolution, Apollonia 6, and The Time—and had them working against you and for you is another testimony to your genius.

*U keep kissing my ass & then kicking my ass.*

Doing neither. Just setting out the story like I see it. Morris in the movie accepted the role as the cool fool. The comic foil. It's not a role to sneeze at. I love comic characters. Love 'em all from Red Foxx to Richard Pryor to Dave Chappelle. I'm not putting myself in their category. I'm a musician before anything. But like Cab Calloway with his "Minnie the Moocher" or Screamin' Jay Hawkins comin' out the coffin to sing "You Put a Spell on Me," I understood how comedic elements could enhance my act.

I also understood how the tension between the real me and the movie me could enhance a story in which the movie me and the movie Prince were at each other's throats. You put on a double whammy on our real-life story by casting yourself as the underdog who has to knock off Morris's crown. At the start of the film, the Morris character has everything; at the end, nothing. The Kid is crowned Prince.

*But u dug it. I remember u at the premiere. U were glowing.*

Cause I was thrilled by how much screen time I got. Then we were all stoked when the premiere audience responded with a standing O. Fans ate it up. But something else happened at that screening that took me completely by surprise.

*What?*

I saw another character emerge. Someone who was me and also not me. Someone whose voice needs to be heard in this book.

*Last thing this book needs is another character with another voice. We already got u & we already got me. Enough's enough.*

It's not enough. This other character's gotta speak for himself. I can't shut him up.

*Who are u talking about?*

MD's got some shit to say.

# 12

# MD

Morris is the cat sitting at the premiere. **MD** is the cat in the movie.

**I'm thinking I'm cool because I am cool. I'm thinking I'm slick because I am slick. I see Morris as laid-back, a cat who's sometimes insecure about what he can and cannot do. But me, MD, hell, I do whatever I wanna do. I wanted to stay high while making this movie and I did. High as a motherfucker. I wanted to play the clown and steal some of the Kid's thunder and yes, sir, I pulled it off. I can float above whatever fears Morris might have. I can live out whatever fantasies Morris doesn't have the balls to fulfill. Seeing me up there on the giant screen larger than life in living Technicolor makes me realize I'm badder than bad.**

**I'm feeling entitled. Cocaine blows up that feeling even more. Cocaine is the fuel that has me excited about the possibilities ahead. Cocaine is telling me that the world is mine.**

*& I was telling u that you're a damn fool.*

**Hard to listen to a man who don't listen to no one but himself.**

*Especially hard when coke's turning your mind 2 mush.*

My mind was clear enough to where I made a third Time album.

*With my help, my song titles, my production. Besides, there was enough of Morris—the Morris who wasn't caught up in insane ego-tripping—2 make that third album right. If this MD character had been in charge, the whole thing might have gone up in smoke.*

Agreed.

MD wasn't in control of those sessions. But neither was I. Prince ran the show, and at this point I wasn't ready to fight the power.

Fans ate up the third Time album, which dropped the same year as *Purple Rain*. Prince called it *Ice Cream Castles*. To show you how complacent I was about letting him lead the way, I didn't even question the title. Just sounded cool. Only recently did I learn—some thirty-five years after its release!—that the title comes from Joni Mitchell's "Both Sides Now." (Joni wrote about rows and flows of angel hair and ice cream castles in the air.) Like I said, Prince was into Joni; I wasn't. Yet, unbeknownst to me, it was Joni's happy phrase that caught on. Turned out to be the right title 'cause the castles started dripping and melting sooner than any of us thought. The title tune is about falling in love in the summertime; it's about feeling young and free.

The two songs from the film were breakout hits: "Jungle Love" and "The Bird," my weird invention. The single for "The Bird" was a live version we'd done at First Avenue just before filming *Purple Rain*. It's unusual that a live recording becomes a single. Stevie Wonder had done it with "Fingertips" twenty years earlier, a song that kicked off his monumental career. I guess we were hoping for the same thing. Listening to the live version, we knew it couldn't be improved upon.

We also knew that *Ice Cream Castles* was essentially a Prince record. I was still heartbroken over the loss of Jimmy Jam and Terry Lewis. Without them, The Time wasn't The Time. Credits read produced by "Morris Day and the Starr," and although Morris Day had lots of input, wrote a lot of the songs, and sang all the leads, the Starr sat in the driver's seat. In the song, for example, called "If the Kid Can't Make You Come (No One Can)," the Kid was obviously the Starr, who was obviously Prince boasting about his orgasm-producing expertise. I stood in as his alter ego, a role I both relished and resented.

*U didn't resent it when* Ice Cream Castles *went double platinum.*

Only when the *Purple Rain* soundtrack went twenty-five times platinum. But we've been over that territory before.

*Good 2 lose resentments. Good 2 work your way thru 'em.*

That's the purpose of this book.

*I c u dwelling on 'em.*

I'm moving on. Just like I did in real life. After *Ice Cream Castles,* I wanted to go solo.

*& I wanted 2 help u do that.* Purple Rain *had established u as your own man. I'd set u up 2 b a solo artist.*

Let's break that shit down. When I went to management to propose the idea of going solo, they said sure, but we better check with Prince. When they checked with you, you also said sure. Except for one thing. You'd maintain creative control.

*& y not? That was the smart move—4 u & me. History has proven me right.*

Maybe. But my view of history is things happen 'cause they're supposed to happen. And it just happened that I had to break away from you. I had to see what kind of songwriter, singer, and producer I could be. I had to follow my own inner voice.

*Don't start getting New Age on me now.*

I ain't talkin' no hocus-pocus. I'm just saying I wanted to be my own man, not Prince's puppet.

*Which was when u got into serious doo-doo. U gonna write about that?*

**He got no choice. I'll be telling those stories. I love those stories. Be a lie to say I didn't love getting high.**

*MD ain't lyin'.*

Never said he was.

In fact, at some point MD took over my life.

*So u've found a way 2 blame someone besides yourself.*

Not trying to do that. MD is me. I claim him and he claimed me. We the same.

*Then y give him a different voice?*

Because that's how I heard him in my head. He spoke to me differently. He convinced me to keep doing shit the other part of my brain knew was bad. But his voice was convincing—at least convincing enough to lure me away from reason.

*You're making him the villain.*

No.

*Well, then, you're making* me *the villain.*

You ain't reading this right. You still paranoid. Out the gate, I been saying I wouldn't have no story were it not for you. Tired of saying that. Just like I was tired of having you run my life and run the life of the band.

So I made up my mind to move on. End of one story and beginning of another.

# 13

# THE SPLIT

Since Prince and I both believed in Jesus, you'd think a come-to-Jesus meeting between the two of us would have been easy to arrange. It wasn't. Later in his life Prince was eager to talk about Jesus with me—and he did—but at this point open communications with his underlings wasn't how he operated. He operated in the shadows. I don't mean he was sinister. I do mean that he was distant. I couldn't just stroll over to his house and talk about my need to go my own creative way. He set it up so all such discussions went through management. Then management would talk to Prince, who would get back to management, who, in turn, would get back to me. Prince lived his life insulated by buffer zones. In years to come, when everyone had a cell phone, he claimed not to have one. He made it impossible to reach him directly.

Before our post–*Purple Rain* falling-out, our relationship had already begun to fray. While the two of us were working on *Ice Cream Castles*, he was living in a Beverly Hills mansion and I was close by at the Westwood Marquis near UCLA. Prince was always running in and out of town and, given our long friendship, gave me carte blanche to drop by whenever I wanted. Sometimes he was there, sometimes not, but I was always made to feel welcome.

On a lonely Los Angeles evening, I was feeling restless and decided to head over to Prince's and see what was shaking. Rode over in my rented Benz. Top down. Starry sky. Neon night. The city was buzzing.

**I was buzzed. Loved that buzz. That buzz brightens all the colors. Chasing the buzz, catching the buzz, watching it slip away, and then chasing it some more. Let's chase that buzz.**

I pulled up to the gate and punched in the magic numbers. The gate slowly opened, allowing me to cruise in and park next to a Rolls Silver Cloud.

Door was unlocked. Party under way. Four of Prince's sexiest sexies were lounging around the living room.

"Morris is here!" shouted one, all smiles.

"Looking sharp, MD," said another with an even bigger smile.

I appreciated being appreciated, and when it came to these friendly ladies, I was doing some deep appreciation of my own.

The chitchat was easy, the vibe relaxed, the TV tuned to Prince videos. Since I had long broken up with Jennifer, I was free as a bird. One of the chicks asked me to sit next to her on the couch. Another sat herself down at my feet. Wasn't sure what would happen next but I felt like I was in the right place at the right time.

Then Prince arrived. The vibe switched up in a second. He stared at me and said, "What are you doing here?"

"Hanging."

"This isn't your house to hang in. Get out."

Just. Like. That.

Man, I was wounded. Didn't even answer back. At this point we'd been through a lot together. At different times we had even dated the same chicks. In spite of that, when it came to the ladies there had never been a cross word between us. Not even back in the Grand Central days. This was something new. Something cruel.

I got out, went back to my hotel, and stewed.

**It was a good reason to get even more buzzed.**

My mind went back to a day during the Dirty Mind Tour when Prince had brought out one of his honeys to parade in front of me. It was after hours in his hotel room and she was half dressed. Blissfully, shamelessly sexy. Not to mention sweet. Prince gave me every indication I should make a move.

*That's your interpretation.*

This whole goddamn book is my interpretation.

*That's the problem.*

There was no problem 'cause when I did make a move and Wonder Woman was willing, Prince seemed pleased. He gave me the idea that when it came to female companionship, he was more than happy to share his good fortune. A few weeks later, though, I was in a hotel suite with Wonder Woman and a couple of other chicks. We were all just having a few giggles, nothing heavy, when the phone rang. Prince was in the lobby wanting to know whether Wonder Woman was up there. He was on the verge of hysteria.

*Exaggeration.*

Says you. I say you were acting like I'd kidnapped her. You didn't like the fact that she and I were together. I explained that there were other party people in our suite. Naturally I invited you up. You responded by slamming down the phone. Wonder Woman ran off to meet you in the lobby. That was the last time I saw her.

Here's another superstrange scenario: During that same tour, you asked me to apply makeup to your back. All this was happening when I had not yet been granted my position as musician. I was still your videographer. Still a gofer. I didn't see myself refusing any reasonable requests. Was this request reasonable?

*Don't make it seem like something it wasn't.*

I didn't know what to make of it. Still don't. All I can say is that it gave me the creeps. I didn't know whether I was being teased, tempted, or tortured. We never discussed it.

*Nothing 2 discuss.*

Except that I was made to feel like your valet.

*Until u got famous with your own valet.*

But even when I had The Time, even when I became the bandleader, even when I unexpectedly was given the main supporting role in *Purple Rain*, a certain cloud hung over me. That cloud was darkened by my drug use. I make no excuse for that. I was doing shit I shouldn't have done.

*U gonna tell about that time u came by my house lyin' 'bout how u needed money for your brother when I knew damn well it was dope money u were after?*

I'm telling it. I'm spilling it out. I remember the night like it was yesterday.

Don't think we'd even wrapped up the *Purple Rain* shoot. I'd eaten through all my bread. A storm was blowing through Minneapolis. The falling snow wasn't the kind of snow I wanted. I wanted blow.

**This ain't a story you gotta tell. This was a bad time. There were good times, good highs, fun highs, highs that blissed out all the lows. Let's talk about those times.**

This was one time I couldn't forget. I was out of money and knew the one place I could get it. So I got dressed, slipped on my pimp shoes, and headed out. In my hurry, I forgot to put on socks. No matter. I drove over to your place. To get from my car to the house meant trudging through two feet of snow. My sockless feet got soaked. No matter, I made it to your front door.

*U looked wasted.*

I *was* wasted. As I sat in front of you, I felt like a fool. Especially when I crossed my legs and saw you noticing my frozen ankles and waterlogged Stacy Adamses. You asked me what I wanted. I made up a lie about my brother being in trouble and me needing $400 to help him out. Your manager Steve Fargnoli was there. He looked at me like I'd just robbed a bank. You were also skeptical as a motherfucker.

*I knew what was happenin'.*

But you gave me the money. I appreciated that.

*That's what they call enabling. I'm not proud of that moment.*

Me either.

**You ain't telling the whole truth. You ran to the dope man. The dope man gave you the relief you was looking for. You did it. You dug it.**

I dug a deep hole. I saw myself falling in that hole. During that long winter I saw myself coming apart. I knew I needed to make a move. I needed to make many moves. The first was to get out of Dodge.

# 14

# WHAT COLOR IS SUCCESS?

Although I had made a mess of myself in Minneapolis, I somehow got it together in LA, where I was clean.

**For a hot minute—and a hot minute only.**

I had no notion of rebuilding The Time. Or any other band. Like I said before, I hate when bands lose their original lineups. Hated losing Jimmy Jam and Terry Lewis. Also hated learning that Jesse Johnson, while still in The Time, had gone off and done a whole album for A&M on his own without saying a word to me. At this point I put all the bands in my life in the past.

The future looked good. One of Hollywood's leading managers wanted to sign me. This happened at a time when I was still under contract to Prince's management—which meant I was still controlled by Prince. He wanted a Morris Day record, but the same way he had wanted a record by The Time, Vanity 6, and Apollonia 6. He wanted to control it. He could reject any song I wrote, any production technique I employed, any mix I made. That was too much for me.

So when Sandy Gallin came along, I was ready for my release. Sandy was Mr. Mogul. His client list included everyone from Dolly Parton to Cher to Whoopi Goldberg. In a few years, he'd be managing Michael Jackson. Sandy saw me as a solo artist. That's all I needed to hear. Beyond his words, he got results. He set up my deal at Warner Brothers, who granted me the right to produce. Only one drawback: To get out of the legal entanglement with Prince, I'd have to pay $300,000. I didn't understand where those numbers came from. I didn't even remember what contracts I had signed. All that's on me. Young artists have the responsibility to take care of business. I didn't.

Truth is, even after signing with Sandy, I still wasn't really sober.

**Now you're talkin'. I was waitin' for you to tell the truth.**

When I went to his office and took meetings with Warner Brothers, the actor in me put on a good act. I came on as Mr. Clean. But I wasn't.

I was living in Los Angeles, holed up in a rental house, and my drug use escalated to where I couldn't hide it from Sandy Gallin. He and his associate Barry Josephson, who handled my day-to-day details, witnessed my steady decline. During the recording of that first solo album, *The Color of Success*, I stormed out of the studio, angry about something I can't even remember. Coke had me on a razor-blade edge. Gallin and Josephson stepped in to save me. They insisted I get help. I was resistant. When they tried to make me go to rehab, like Amy Winehouse, I said no, no, no.

**You had no intention of ever stopping. You said yes to rehab only to placate those Hollywood big shots.**

No argument there. I didn't really care about sobriety. I only cared about not losing Sandy Gallin and Barry Josephson. I still cared about my career. So I agreed to check into a UCLA rehab facility, one of the best in the country.

**I turned it into a joke.**

I went to individual psychotherapy, group therapy sessions, and twelve-step meetings.

**They were all jokes.**

And I'd sneak out to get wasted in some hideaway club in Hollywood.

**That buzz. You still wanted that fuckin' buzz.**

I cut up, fucked up, and broke up every good plan set out before me. All the time, though, I managed to pretend that I was going along with a program that I was secretly undermining.

After a month, I was sent home, where things got worse. Snorting coke is one thing; smoking the shit is another thing entirely.

**If one buzz is strong, maybe a different buzz will be stronger. That's how the high life works.**

Couldn't admit it at the time, but that's how death works. The pipe is death. The pipe makes you shut your bedroom door and do nothing but smoke your brains out. I was in the process of doing that very thing when the two strongest women in my life came by and broke down the door. Mom and sister Sandy. They wouldn't stand by and let me die in darkness. They literally got me out of the bed and into the sunlight. They knew my last rehab was bullshit and said so. When my mother, with tears running down her cheeks, said, "You're wasting your life away," I started crying as well.

Sandy Gallin had influence over me. He represented hope for my emerging solo career. But Sandy Gallin's influence did not stop me from fucking up that first rehab. Sandy Gallin didn't have the power to straighten out my crooked ass. Mom did. Sister Sandy did. They were talking about more than a professional future; they were talking life and death.

"It's simple," said sister Sandy. "Go to rehab or go to your grave."

**I didn't like that ultimatum.**

I did. Your voice was strong, but sister Sandy's voice was even stronger.

I went to rehab, but a different one than UCLA. My second therapy was tougher. It was also effective. It employed aversion therapy. Never had heard the term before. Wasn't sure what to expect. I soon learned that it was more than psychotherapy. Psychotherapy is fine, but in those sessions I'm not much of a talker. I withdraw. This new therapy involved a medical routine that did more than block the good-feeling effects of a coke high. The aversion medicine changed my body chemistry so that even the thought of cocaine made me sick to my stomach. I retched. I thought I was going to die. The sickness, retching, and thoughts of death busted my steely stubborn streak. I broke down. And because I broke down, I found a way to build myself back up. I was reminded—and still remind myself every day—that a force greater than myself is at work in the world. You can call that force Jesus, God, a higher power, or just pure love. All those names are good—names that I said aloud during this second rehab.

Might have also helped that this facility, unlike the first, was outside the city. It was up at Lake Arrowhead, where, among the pine trees, blue water, and clear sky, the air was fresh. Nature was in my face. And nature became another way to see a healing God. Miraculously, that rebellious spirit that had me heading off the side of a cliff found peace and quiet in the mountains. Clarity became the aim. Clarity was the gift. Clarity changed everything. I was clear that drugs were blocking my bliss. I'm not saying that all my dramas were over—many more dramas would soon materialize—but thank God I didn't live through those dramas high. Being high would have only made the dramas worse.

**Or better. And for sure a helluva lot more fun.**

The success of this second rehab came roughly at the same time as the birth of my second child, Taj. I had met his mother, Sherry, during a time when I was still ripping and running. Our romance was short-lived. That doesn't mean I didn't care for Sherry. I knew then, and know now, that she'd be a wonderful mother. The birth of our son was a joyful moment. I did care for him financially, but Sherry had wisely formed a life without me. She had the fortitude to become a responsible single mother. I wish I could have been closer to Taj when he was growing up. I never stop beating myself up for not being there for all my children all the time. I have no excuses. Only regrets.

As a father, I was not a great success.

I called my first solo album *The Color of Success*. The cover showed me on a balcony dressed in a black overcoat, red suit, and white scarf with the neon rainbow of Times Square below me. Thinking back, I probably should have called the record *The Colors of Success*, plural. Now I know that success has many shades. . . .

*Do we really have 2 hear your philosophy? Do u have 2 come off like some wise guru?*

Ain't acting like no guru. Just saying that, at age twenty-nine, I thought success was nothing but a series of green lights. Anchors away. Full steam ahead. I didn't know that inside those green lights the blues were hiding. Didn't know that success meant dealing with some blues I'd never met before. But there were also beautiful shades, radiant colors that lit up my life. Given my battle with drugs, I saw the act of completing *The Color of Success* as a success.

*It was hardly a megasuccess. Don't u b bragging.*

Wasn't gonna brag at all. I knew you wouldn't allow that. Looking back, I'm just amazed that the album isn't half bad. It was my effort to write, sing, and produce every track. I had help from first-rate keyboardists like Greg Phillinganes, who'd been one of Quincy Jones's main men on Michael's *Off the Wall* and *Thriller*. One reviewer wrote that my "huge personality" brought the tracks to life. He reminded his readers that I was still trading on the MD character from *Purple Rain* and still working inside The Time machine mold responsible for hits like "Jungle Love." He wasn't wrong. At that point, the MD character was all I had. I wasn't about to play down his swag or undermine his image.

**Least I get some props.**

The record did, in fact, yield a hit, "The Oak Tree," a follow-up dance to "The Bird" where, rooted in fertile funk, I grow strong and spread my branches. It was a metaphor of hope for my future.

*Well, I'm gonna say something I never said 2 your face. I dug that song. I was proud of u 4 putting out that record.*

Love hearing that, bro. Means the world to me. Back then, I heard through the grapevine that's how you felt. But when "The Oak Tree" dropped and started making noise, you were out there with Sheila E. doing a bit about how your big ol' ax was gonna cut down the oak tree. Y'all were fucking with me.

*All in good fun. U gotta keep your humor, Morris. U gotta remember that when I did "Pop Life," it was a cautionary tale. I was talkin' 'bout u 'cause I cared.*

I heard that. I knew that I was that character in "Pop Life" snorting shit up his nose. I knew you wanted to help me. I also knew a song was your only way of getting a message across. You weren't about to call me.

*I don't remember getting any calls from u.*

We were going down different paths. You were going off with Sheila E. while I was about to go off with a new woman.

Love awaited me. But love, at least in my life, has never arrived without complications.

# 15

# THE CHARACTER

*Guess I'm just a victim, girl,*
*Victim of society*
*Guess I'm a character*
*At least that's what people say*
*Eyes of expectations*
*Look beyond reality*
*Just to be original*
*Doesn't come so easily*
*Guess you'd call it image, girl*
*Or maybe personality*
*I guess you'd call it character*
*Wanted by society*
*Maybe what you're seeing is a bit of grandiosity*
*Or just an image of what you'd like for me to be*
*I'm not sure, but if it works for you*
*It works for me*
*I'm just a victim, girl,*
*Scared to fall in love*
*I'm just a character*
*Scared of love.*

"The Character" was the song from *The Color of Success* that best expressed the confusion in my heart and head. The confusion was profound. I had fallen into victim mentality. As the song says, I felt like the victim of people's expectations. I had to live up to my image as a playa/cutup/cool cat.

**That's me. That's the dude folks like. He makes 'em laugh. He makes 'em sing and dance and get happy. Don't trash that dude.**

I couldn't trash him. I had to be him. Had to display grandiosity because grandiosity—looking in that mirror and liking what I saw—was part of the act. I admit that I wasn't sure the act was working. Inside, I was feeling hollow. But I wasn't looking to myself for validation. I was looking to the public. That's why I said if this act works for you, it works for me.

I write instinctively and freely. When I composed "The Character," those words just poured out of me. No prethought, no postanalysis, just spontaneity. Reading those lyrics thirty-three years later is a trip. It reveals the turmoil I was going through. It was my mind-set while I was getting my show together to tour behind *The Color of Success.*

I was not in the MD role of "The Character" when I was auditioning background singers.

**You sure 'bout that? Sure you weren't doing the ol' casting-couch bit?**

Very sure. There was no couch. It was just me in a rehearsal studio listening carefully to singers. I was looking for vocal excellence. I was not looking for love. But when one of the women began to sing, I felt love. I can't explain it. It had never happened to me before. It was more than the fine quality of her voice or the beauty of her fine face and figure. It was love. After she had gone through two numbers I turned to my piano player and said words that sounded absolutely crazy. "I'm going to marry that woman," I said.

Her name was Judith Jones. Her résumé was exemplary. She had studied cello and piano. She had been a *Soul Train* dancer. She'd sung background on Earth, Wind & Fire's I Am Tour. She had also worked extensively with Lou Rawls. I later learned about her family. Her father was not only an accomplished musician but the first African American engineer hired by NASA. Her mother was principal of a middle school. Judi was far more educated than me, more articulate, and more astute about worldly matters.

During her audition I didn't know any of these things. I just heard something inside me say, "Get next to her, stay next to her, don't let her get away."

Fortunately, Judi felt the same. I'm glad to report that her feelings weren't for MD because she wasn't familiar with my work. Like the rest of the world, she knew and admired Prince but was only vaguely familiar with The Time. I liked that. I liked that she wasn't a fan and hadn't bought into the hype.

Word travels fast, and I'd been hearing for some time that Prince was not thrilled that I'd left his camp. . . .

*I told u I was proud of u. . . .*

More pissed than proud. I say that 'cause when you made your second movie you were quick to pluck Jerome Benton out of my entourage and put him in yours. That meant, of course, that Jerome wouldn't be touring with me. Jerome was no longer my sidekick. He was your sidekick. You were letting me know that you didn't need me.

Your new movie, *Under the Cherry Moon*, was a film you directed and starred in. It was also a movie where you partially played me. Later I heard rumors that the original follow-up to *Purple Rain* planned by Prince was supposed to be *The Adventures of Morris and Jerome*.

*It was just a fleeting thought. I have lots of fleeting thoughts.*

But you took that thought and instead of playing yourself, you played me.

**You mean me.**

Yes. Prince played the MD character from *Purple Rain*, the character he'd created. In other words, he was playing his alter ego. To put the cherry on the cake, he recruited Jerome to be his foil. To be honest, I couldn't get through the whole movie. I'm no film critic and I'm not here to groove on Prince's missteps. . . .

*I wonder about that. . . .*

I'm really not. I could go on about the many beyond-brilliant albums you'd make in the coming decades. Your work ethic never stopped, not for a second. And the hard work paid off in a song catalog so big we're still discovering new songs. Your music will be around forever.

*Every time u build me up, I'm looking for the hammer 2 beat me down.*

Ain't no beat-downs. Just issues to address. I understood what was going through your mind with *Cherry Moon*. *Purple Rain* had gone through the roof. Megahit. And all your idea. You were the driving force behind it. You were burning up the industry. Only reasonable to think that now you could do it all by yourself. With *Purple Rain* you'd had partial control. Its success gave you the confidence to take total control of *Cherry Moon*. You were gutsy. You were thinking, "Why shoot another movie in freezing-ass Minneapolis? Why not go to the south of France? Why not shoot it on the Riviera, the most glamorous spot in Europe? And why not make myself up to look like Rudolph Valentino?"

There's a resemblance between you and Rudolph, I admit, but casting yourself as a gigolo hitting on European honeys got boring. Also got boring watching you go for the comedy routines I did with Jerome. I heard you saying, "I don't need MD. I can do what MD did—and then some."

*U r hearing things in your head that I never said. I was just trying 2 make a movie that was half funny, half romantic.*

Come on, bro. You were over your head, but no one could or would tell you that. They were scared of you. I wasn't. Had I been around, I would have said something. I would have said that you and Jerome proposing a ménage à trois with some chick was a little freaky. I'm not happy the film flopped. All I'm saying is that I wasn't surprised when no one went to see it.

*Here's what I say: The film was an experiment. Not all experiments work. But all artists gotta keep experimenting. 2 other points b4 u trash it even worse. On the soundtrack 4* Under the Cherry Moon *was a little song called "Kiss." #1 all over the world. Then 3 years later, when Tom Jones covered it, #1 all over again. 1 last point: on the soundtrack I also used the superclassy arranger Clare Fischer. If I remember correctly u took the cue & used Clare 4 your next solo record.*

I was always paying attention to you, always learning from you, but that doesn't mean I didn't see when you were going off course. *Cherry Moon* was way off course.

*& r u sure that the fact that u r not in the movie didn't shade your attitude?*

No, 'cause I can say truthfully that even though I was in the next film you made—*Graffiti Bridge*—I felt the same.

*We gotta go there?*

Not now. 'Cause now my mind is on the start of my family with Judi Jones. It was the opening of a brand-new chapter.

# 16

# DAYDREAMING

They once asked Marvin Gaye what, more than anything, he wanted in life. "Simple domestic happiness" was all he said.

I relate. I was after the same thing. A good woman. Kids. Solid home. Financial security. A chance to make good music. And no drama. Sounds easy. And attainable. But to tell you the truth, very few of my colleagues have reached that goal.

Not hard to figure out why. Stardom isn't healthy for your head. You confuse the man on the stage with the man off the stage.

*U were confused. Not everyone is. Sometimes the man on the stage & off the stage r the same.*

I don't believe it.

*I do.*

**I do too.**

But how the hell can you tell if the offstage man remains hidden? No one really knew what you were thinking or what you were doing until you did it.

*It came out in my work. It's all my work. It's all clear.*

Only if we go back over your work and figure out how it all hangs together. But if I do that, you'll accuse me of being overanalytical. You'll say I'm reading into your songs shit that isn't there.

*U don't have 2 do anything but listen 2 it. Y analyze it? Y still try & figure it out?*

Cause that's what human beings do. We think.

*Think 2 much. Way 2 much.*

**I'm thinking the same. Too much thinking don't do no one no good.**

I'm just thinking about myself. Thinking how when I met Judi I knew I'd found what I'd been looking for. A brilliant chick. A chick who was musical and, yes, thoughtful and understanding. We got married in 1986. It's no accident that while I was making my second solo album, the one I called *Daydreaming*, Judi was pregnant with our first child. Dreams were coming true.

Judi was the first to see that the man on and off the stage was two separate beings. That worried her. She wasn't shy to express that worry.

**Worried me too. She thought too much. If I was gonna get any action, I could see her getting in my way.**

Judi believed in Morris, not MD.

She was a person who *did* believe in analyzing multilayered emotions. She believed in therapy. Yet therapy worried me. I didn't want no stranger getting into my business. In that regard, I was with my man Prince. Don't look too deeply behind the facade. It's taken a long time to craft that facade. The facade, in fact, is a work of art. The facade is making money and bringing me something I find alluring and maybe even irresistible: adoration.

**Adoration is my middle name. I love it. The higher I get, the more adoration I crave. Fact is, adoration makes the high even higher.**

That's another reason stars get fucked up. They're adored. It's okay to be adored by your woman or children or your mother and father. Okay to be adored by your friends. But to be adored by a world of worshipful fans—that ain't real good for your mental health. For sure, it feels good at the time. Who doesn't want to see a stadium filled with people screaming your name, dancing to your grooves, and calling for more? You feel like a god. But your hungry ego sneaks its way into that feeling of adoration and whispers into your ear. . . .

**You're entitled to everything. You work your ass off. You bring people music they love. You bring them pleasure. Artistically, you give them all they want. In return, you can have whatever *you* want. You've earned it. Besides, the culture condones it. Stars are expected to have their indulgences. Stars are forgiven those indulgences. Goes with the territory. So go on and ego-trip because without your ego you would never have achieved stardom. Stardom is ego. Stardom is MD. The more stardom, the more ego, the more adoration, the more fun.**

The whole thing scrambles the mind. At least it scrambled my mind. It scrambles the minds of most stars.

*Speak 4 yourself.*

I am. I'm confessing that it was with a scrambled mind that I made *Daydreaming*. I was still eager to show the world that I could be a star on my own.

*But u were already a star.* Purple Rain *made u a star.*

You keep saying that, and maybe it was true. But I wasn't feeling it. I was feeling I still had something to prove. Besides, the music inside me still needed to come out. And I wanted it expressed the best way possible. That's why I reached back to Jimmy Jam and Terry Lewis. A year earlier they'd become the hottest producers on the planet with Janet Jackson. After being fired from The Time, they right away started doing good work. They had big R&B hits with the SOS Band, Alexander O'Neal, and Cherrelle—just to mention a few. But their work with Janet broke the bank. The Janet/Jam and Lewis album, *Control*, put her on the map. She recorded it in Minneapolis, where Jimmy and Terry brought out her true sweet-salty-sparkling personality. They gave her dazzling dance grooves that inspired her lyrics declaring her freedom. The whole thing was beautiful. And funky. So funky, in fact, that Prince felt a little threatened.

*Here u go again. . . .*

You're saying it ain't true that you drove over to Jimmy Jam's house blasting out a track and yelling, "Can you make it funkier than this?"

*& if u ask Jimmy Jam, he'll say that only inspired him 2 cut even funkier tracks. He'll say it was my spirit that pushed him & Terry 2 do what they did.*

We'll all say that. We'll all say you were the one who said find another harmony part when we thought we had the harmonies covered. You were the one who made us learn choreography moves until we dropped from exhaustion. It was you who taught us to put together a mind-blowing stage show.

But I believe that after we learned all that shit from you, you got a little crazy. When you saw how good we'd gotten—whether it was me, Jimmy Jam, or Terry—you freaked out. The freak-out came when you thought maybe, just maybe, you'd be outshone. We had too much regard for you to see that possibility, but maybe you did.

*Then y would I put u, Jimmy Jam & Terry in* Graffiti Bridge*?*
*Y would I put u back in the spotlight?*

I'll get to that. I'm not there yet.

*You're dragging.*

I'm the drummer. I'm putting the pocket where it needs to be.

*I'm also a drummer. & I'm saying u way behind the beat.*

The beat slows down when I'm talking about a record like *Daydreaming*.

*A record with some good cuts. But a record the world's forgotten.*

Not entirely. You forget that *Daydreaming* had me back playing with the cats. Jimmy Jam and Terry Lewis, between *Control* and *Rhythm Nation*, took off time from Janet and wrote and produced two songs, a beautiful ballad, "Love Is a Game," and the sexy "Fishnet," which was an R&B hit. On those tracks, Jellybean was back on drums, Jesse Johnson on guitar, and Jerome doing backgrounds.

I was also writing more introspectively, especially on one song I called "A Man's Pride."

*I heard "A Man's Pride" & dug it. But like I said b4, I also saw how u used my man Clare Fischer.*

Your man Fischer was writing for the Jacksons before he was writing for you. You hardly discovered him. He was a great arranger. His chart for "A Man's Pride" brought out the power of my lyrics:

*When you're young you make mistakes*
*That tend to leave you sad*
*As you grow you learn to take*
*The good things with the bad*

*Cause it takes a man*
*Just to understand a man's pride*
*As a man it all begins*
*to change your point of view*
*And it seems it never ends*
*The things you're going through*

*To make the sacrifice*
*The price you had to pay*
*Only worth as much as*
*You learn along the way*

*Cause it takes a man*
*Just to understand a man's pride*

*It's a man's pride*
*Makes him laugh*
*It makes him cry*
*It's a man's pride that keeps a man alive*

I look at those words and wonder what was going through my mind when I approved the album. I say that because the *Daydreaming* cover photo had me fantasizing about my own jet, a fancy car, and a super-sexy lady—all the elements that made me prideful.

**The elements that make me happy.**

Yet the song itself goes in a different direction. I was trying to get beyond a superficial understanding of what it means to be a man. I was trying to understand the difference between puffed-up pridefulness and genuine pride. When I was high on drugs, that distinction didn't exist. It was all about staying high. All about staying in a state of blissed-out fog.

**A state you loved.**

Yes, but when the fog finally lifted, I began to see that pride—true pride—was necessary to craft the kind of songs that mattered. "A Man's Pride" mattered. It put the subject on the table. It said I had done things in my younger life that made me sad. I had ruined romantic relationships before they had a chance to blossom. Before Judi, I had never been true to one woman. And yet I understood that whatever mistakes I had made, I required pride—pride to pursue dreams beyond surface thrills.

*Daydreaming* dropped in 1987. Our son Evan was born in July of that year. I was overjoyed. I knew that Judi would handle motherhood beautifully—and she did.

At the start of 1988, we started off the Daydreaming Tour in London before bringing it back to the States. The crowds were enthusiastic. "Fishnet" was in heavy rotation on MTV. On the video, Jimmy Jam, Jellybean, Jerome, and Terry had my back. We had a ball. We were rolling.

So was Prince. *Daydreaming* dropped around the same time as his *Sign o' the Times*. A friend of mine always reminds me of the danger of "compare and despair." If I compare the commercial/critical reception of *Daydreaming* to *Sign o' the Times*, I will despair. Prince's record generated three top-ten hits—the title cut, "U Got the Look," and "I Could Never Take the Place of Your Man." This was his first project after breaking up the Revolution and proving, once again, that he was only getting better. Strangely enough, though, I didn't really despair all that much. Prince and I had been running in different lanes. I was proud of the work I'd done. I wish I hadn't clung so tightly, at least in terms of the cover photo, to the MD of *Purple Rain*, but I still saw that as my calling card.

Meanwhile, more than ever, Prince's calling card was sex.

*I wouldn't say that.*

I just did. How else you gonna explain that your album right after *Sign o' the Times* was *Lovesexy*? On the cover, you were stark naked, sitting on a bed of oversized white and purple lilies.

*That wasn't the 1st idea.*

I know. You told me you wanted to put out *The Black Album* with an all-black cover. But you dumped it.

*I decided 2 make a different point.*

Which was?

*Ain't no shame in my game.*

And what's the game?

*Expression of myself. All my self. Full disclosure. Full exposure. Nothing 2 hide.*

The mystique was still there. You took off your clothes, but that don't mean you took off your mask.

*Fool, I took off everything.*

You say no shame in your game, but to me the game was the same we'd all been playing since back in the day. Get noticed. Get bigger gigs. Attract bigger audiences. And hypersexy music illustrated by hypersexy images was still your way of doing all that.

*& u weren't?*

I was. I just didn't do it as well as you. I was still the student. Hell, I will always be the student. But there did come a time, right after *Lovesexy* didn't perform as well as you liked, that the student came to the teacher with something the teacher liked.

Lovesexy *went gold.*

Gold ain't platinum. You were never happy with anything less than platinum. And you sure as hell weren't happy when it became your first album since the early '80s not to hit the top ten. Maybe that's why you were so receptive when I came to you.

*I was always happy 2 hear your ideas, Morris. Besides, u still hadn't seen Paisley Park. I knew u were dying 2 c it.*

No doubt.

*So I invited u back home. U'd been out in LA 2 long. It was time 2 reconnect 2 your roots.*

You make it sound easy.

*It was.*

Let me break it down so the people can see for themselves.

Showin' off my
early good looks
(Springfield, 1956)

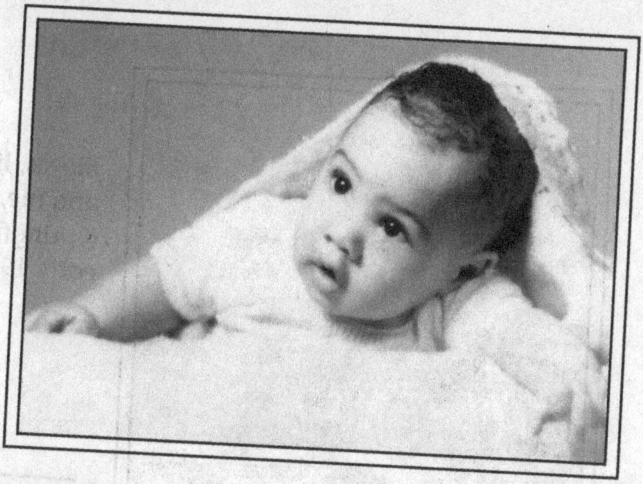

Me and big
sis chillin' in
the backyard
(Springfield,
late 1950s)

Lookin' serious and not
missing any meals
(Springfield, late 1950s)

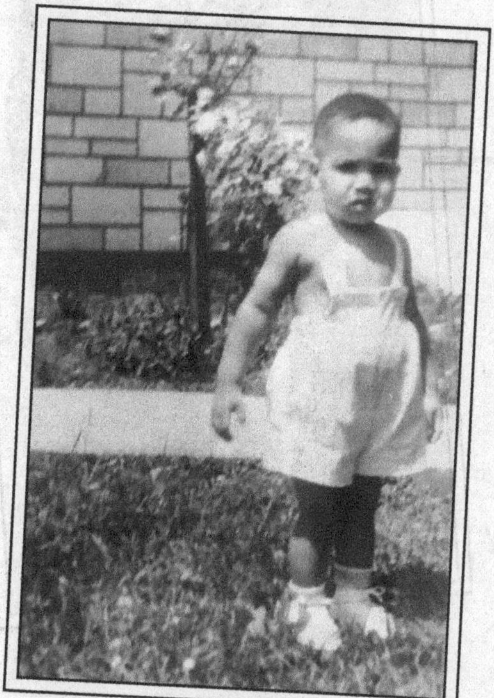

Big sis, little bro, and me, posin' (Springfield, early 1960s)

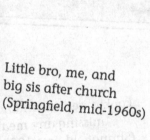

Showin' off the freckles, school pic (Minneapolis, mid-1960s)

Little bro, me, and big sis after church (Springfield, mid-1960s)

Graduation class, sixth grade (Minneapolis, mid-1960s)

The Grand Central Days
(Minneapolis, early 1970s)

Rockin' the 'fro with a few
extra pounds (Minneapolis, 1972)

MD,
seventies fresh,
leather and all
(mid-1970s)

Showin' off some
skills on the skins
(Minneapolis,
mid-1970s)

Surprised by
the camera
(Minneapolis,
early 1980s)

First official photo shoot
(Minneapolis, 1981)

Lookin' too cool
(Minneapolis, 1981)

Rockin' the zoot suit
(Minneapolis, 1981)

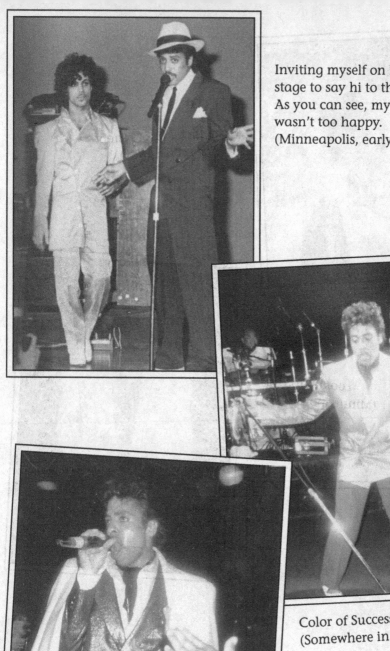

Inviting myself on Prince's stage to say hi to the crowd. As you can see, my man wasn't too happy. (Minneapolis, early 1980s)

Color of Success Tour (Somewhere in the world, 1984)

Solo tour (Somewhere in the world, 1984)

Hanging with sons
Evan and Derran
(Los Angeles, early 1990s)

Me and brother Jesse
(Springfield, late 1990s)

Ladies and gentlemen,
The Time! From left to right:
Jellybean Johnson, Monte Moir,
Jesse Johnson, me, Jerome Benton,
Jimmy Jam, and Terry Lewis (2008)

Me and the one and only Jerome Benton, steppin' up the game (Los Angeles, 2014)

Present day with my lovely wife, Lorena (2019)

# 17

# DON'T I GET MY OWN CHAPTER?

You've already had your say.

**Yeah, but I got more to say. Besides, I was in your life. Then and now.**

I put down the bad stuff. Never would go back to it.

**But you still heard me talking.**

Saying what?

**Saying that drugs ain't the only way to get high. You can always roll up your ego and smoke it. It's another method to take you out of yourself.**

And why would I do that?

**To forget the things about yourself you don't like.**

What things?

**Plenty of things. You never developed your musicianship like you could have. Your dream of being the baddest drummer in the world didn't come true 'cause you stopped practicing.**

Stopped practicing 'cause I had to concentrate on being the lead singer and commanding the stage. Had to make my bones as an entertainer. Besides, even if I had built up my drumming chops, in a few years it wouldn't have made any difference because of computers. The days when master drummers like Harvey Mason could go running from one session to another and make a good living were over. Before I knew it, everyone had learned how to make beats.

**Excuses. Rationalizations. You're also pissed at yourself for not mastering keyboards, guitar, and bass. You just did what you had to do to get by. That made you feel bad about yourself. And when you feel bad about yourself, you call me. MD. MD always provides you with an extra coat of cool. MD covers up a multitude of sins by saying to the world, "Ain't no one gonna get past this pose." MD does for you the same thing you been accusing Prince of doing to himself.**

*I finally got someone who sees my point of view. I think I like this MD better than I like Morris. He's a whole lot tougher on Morris than I ever was.*

**Tougher 'cause I know Morris ain't all that. Morris was run by his mama, and then he was run by his wife, Judi. Morris been hiding behind strong women until those strong women only made him weaker. I'm the only thing that makes him feel strong. I'm his blown-up ego who says, "Fuck it all. Ain't nobody can do what I can do. I'm the motherfuckin' Color of Success.'"**

I already established that wasn't no big success.

**So go on and act like it was. Act like you're some superstar who don't need nobody's help to do nothing.**

I never acted that way. Maybe sometimes I felt that way, but I kept my wits about me.

**All I'm saying is that maybe you didn't get high on coke, but you wanted to get high on something. Something to block out**

**the confusion blowing through your brain. Once an addict, always an addict. That's me. That's MD, the addict side of you that ain't ever gonna stop whispering in your ear. Go a year without getting high. Go two years. Go five years.**

I did.

**You can white-knuckle all you wanna, but that don't shut me up none.**

For all your talk, what are you saying?

**Escape's a beautiful thing. You lookin' to escape yourself. Always have. Always will. And I'm your escape clause. I'm your ticket out. Go out on a drug trip. Go out on an ego trip. Go out on a drinking binge. It all works to make you feel good.**

Until I feel bad.

**Which is when you need more of me to feel good again. The circle stays unbroken.**

I got out of that circle.

**You sure?**

Positive.

**Then why do I keep coming back?**

We all got voices in our heads. And one of the loudest voices—*your* goddamn voice—wants to make us feel bad. Wants us to feel worthless. Don't ask me why. All I know is that voice is always talking about regret. Regretting the past and fearing the future. The voice wants to empty out my confidence and fill it up with shit that will eventually do me in.

I'm not saying I'm capable of turning off the voice completely. MD may pop up again every once in a while. MD wants attention. Like every part of us, MD probably even wants love. But as I got into my thirties, I knew enough not to let MD take the lead.

Morris was the sane one. And Morris knew that part of his sanity was rooted in his relationship to someone who, despite his super-quirky nature, was the kind of artist who comes along only once in a hundred years.

Morris knew to get back with Prince.

# 18

# CORPORATE WORLD

The end of the '80s. Ronald Reagan was on his way out, Bush the First on his way in. In America, it was a Republican world. I looked around and saw how it was also becoming a corporate world. By that I mean that the rebellious and even revolutionary attitudes that started in the '60s and in many ways got even stronger in the '70s turned soft in the '80s. Conformity was on the rise.

Some artists bucked that conformity. With the help of Jam and Lewis, Janet Jackson did her best to rally the troops with *Rhythm Nation*, a record that had a lot to say about the state of the world. A record with a strong social consciousness.

Coincidentally, at the same time that Jimmy and Terry were working with Janet, Jerome Benton and I came up with a song—and an overview for a suite of songs—that addressed some of those same concerns. I was seeing how the American workplace (and the American landscape in general) was choking on its old polluted ideas. Bigotry and racism were on the rise.

Sad to say, thirty years later bigotry and racism are still raging. And to bring things full circle, one of the songs written for *Corporate World* was "Donald Trump (Black Version)." Trump was the avatar of the age. He was famous for his sexual exploits, the media-magnet playboy fucking gorgeous models, the man who had perfected the art of the deal and used any means necessary not to realize social justice but to make himself filthy rich. The black version of Trump doesn't use brain, heart, or even swag to get the girls. He gets them because they can't resist the color green.

Purple, of course, was Prince's color. He was a genius at branding. So I was a little surprised when I pulled up to Paisley Park, situated in the burbs twenty miles south of Minneapolis. The exterior was not painted purple but white. The complex looked like a museum of modern art. It was boxy and big—big enough to hold an entire sound stage, concert venue, and too many studios to count. There were private living quarters and hidden corners everywhere. It was a maze that reflected the mystique of the maestro.

The maestro had sent for me because he'd heard some of the tracks I'd done for *Corporate World* and wanted to hear more. The maestro was eager to renew our friendship and musical relationship. Not that the maestro was waiting for me at the front door. The maestro liked to make entrances and, to build up the drama, the maestro didn't mind keeping you waiting. Even if you were an old buddy. Especially if you were an old buddy.

I was sitting in one of the smaller state-of-the-art studios when the maestro showed up. Prince was always Prince. By that I mean he never showed up in casual threads or, God forbid, something shabby. He showed up in supersharp stage outfits. For our first corporate meeting he was wearing a powder-blue jumpsuit that fit him like a glove. His felt fedora was the same shade of blue.

It had been few years since I'd seen him, but it could have been yesterday.

"Welcome home," he said, friendly as he could be. "How's your mama and them?"

"Doing good, bro. Thanks."

"How's marriage?"

"Beautiful."

And from there, we were off and running. Nothing had changed. Prince was relaxed around me because he sensed I was relaxed around him. Much as I admired him, I wasn't intimidated by his presence. Since so many people were, he appreciated my easy way of talking to him.

He talked about how Miles Davis had come to Paisley and played an invite-only New Year's concert with him. He talked about how he'd done a track for Miles's *Tutu* album. Miles played trumpet over the track but Prince, always a keen critic—especially of his own music—pulled it back because he didn't think it was right for Miles.

"Then why did you send it in the first place?" I asked.

"I didn't know it wouldn't match Miles until Miles went in the studio to test it out."

"Would you ever tour with Miles?" I asked.

"In a heartbeat. He calls, I come running. He's the North Star. He's the Bright One. Bowie talks about Major Tom. Well, I talk about Miles. He's the astronaut furthest out there."

We also talked about Michael Jackson. MJ's *Bad* was out, and Prince told me the story of how Michael wanted Prince to sing on the song and perform on the video. Prince turned him down. That role went to Wesley Snipes.

"Why didn't you do it?" I asked.

"Mike showed me the first line of the song that said, 'Your butt is mine.' I didn't even bother to ask him if he was going to sing that line to me or if I was supposed to sing it to him. Either way, it wasn't gonna happen. And the truth is that he didn't need me. The song was a monster hit without me."

"And the two of you got along?"

"Why shouldn't we? There's no rivalry."

I raised an eyebrow.

"Lower that eyebrow," said Prince. "I make a distinction between healthy competition and rivalry."

"What's the distinction?"

"Someone is a rival only if you think he possesses something you want or need. I'm believing I have everything I want and need. No envy, just admiration."

From there we started talking about this *Corporate World* concept that Prince admired.

After maybe twenty minutes of chopping it up verbally, we started chopping it up musically. He grabbed his guitar, I slid behind a drum kit, and just like that, we were back at it. The grooves came fast and furious. Our chemistry was still cooking. I could see we could knock out this record in no time.

Being back in Prince World was wonderful. Loved making that music. Loved working with the one cat who not only got me but pushed me to outdo myself. Couldn't have been happier until I was reminded of that other aspect of Prince World that ain't so wonderful. Just as Prince will magically appear, he'll just as magically disappear.

*I was a busy man. I was juggling 6 projects at the same time. U r forgetting about* Batman.

Who the fuck could forget about *Batman*? *Batman* was bad. You not only did the soundtrack album but landed the star, Kim Basinger. And you weren't shy about showing her off. At the time she was the First Lady of Paisley Park.

*A lovely lady.*

All your ladies were lovely. Liked them all. Made it my business not to get into your business. My business was to get back into the music business with you. When I left Minneapolis, I felt certain our reconnection was real.

*It was.*

But just as real was your MO. That usually stands for *modus operandi*. In your case, it's the mystery of operation. This time the mystery started when, without warning, you vanished into thin air. You simply didn't show up for our second recording session at Paisley. No one could tell me where you were or, if you were gone, when you'd be back. One of your assistants did tell me, though, that you were serious about our new project and to stand by. I would have preferred to be assured by you, but I took whatever reassurance I could get. I went back to LA.

Judi, baby Evan, and I were living in a townhouse on Olympic Boulevard in Beverly Hills. After my session with Prince in Paisley, I put my plans for a new Morris Day album on hold. I tolerated the frustration of not knowing exactly what was happening because of the possibility of a big payoff. Prince was into *Corporate World*. He was talking about it as a new Morris/Prince combination. That would obviously boost my career. Couldn't wait to return to Minneapolis and complete the record. But fate's a funny thing.

*Gonna get philosophical again?*

Gonna try to make sense of shit that, at the time, made no sense of all. It looked like *Corporate World* was a done deal. At least you said so. But in Prince World collaboration contracts were hardly common. You liked to work on a handshake, a wink, or a nod. Besides, we were such old friends that you and I didn't have to pay lawyers thousands of dollars for written confirmation of something we had already confirmed.

"No doubt about it, Morris," you said. "We're in this thing together."

And we were—except for one thing: The thing kept changing. I thought the thing was *Corporate World*. But as the weeks rolled by, the thing changed. Easily distracted, you had turned your fertile mind back to film. *Cherry Moon* might have flopped, but your *Batman* soundtrack was the bomb. You created the soundtrack album of an international blockbuster. You caught film fever all over again.

While I wanted to make a record, you decided you wanted to make a movie.

*U got the story wrong. Wasn't 1 or the other. It was both.*

It was baffling. It was something I didn't see coming.

You had this notion of not only building a bridge back between me and you but also between you and Jam and Lewis, now the hottest producers in the land because of Janet's *Rhythm Nation*.

The bridge was a great idea and might have been a highlight of all of our careers except for one fact: the bridge collapsed.

# 19

# GRAFFITI BRIDGE

I've supplemented my insufficient education by surrounding myself with some educated friends. One recently was telling me about Ralph Waldo Emerson, the American philosopher famous for his essay "Self-Reliance." I wouldn't be surprised if Prince read it. Emerson says, "Nothing has authority over the self," and I know that's something Prince believed—at least until, years later, he got into his extreme religious bag. Emerson also said, "Trust thyself. Every heart vibrates to that iron string."

Prince had iron-strong trust in himself. He was Mr. Self-Reliant. So much of that was good. His ability to play all instruments got him that singular sound he wanted. Most artists can't produce themselves. He could. Most musicians can't arrange their own charts. He could. Most musicians can't write and direct their own movies. Well, he tried.

I don't fault him for trying. He built Paisley Park, after all, as a self-contained complex to satisfy his need to create his self-reliant projects, movies included. There was a sound stage worthy of high-tech Hollywood. He could fall out of bed and take an elevator down to the set. He could also shape the story he wanted to tell. The story is where the problem began.

*Cherry Moon* didn't have much of a story, and besides, he didn't write it. He suggested it. But it hardly mirrored his life. *Purple Rain*, the surprise success that preceded *Cherry Moon*, did mirror his life. *Purple Rain* also had two characters the public liked—Prince and Morris. Most importantly, *Purple Rain* made a shitload of money, both as a film and as a soundtrack. All that played on Prince's mind as he put *Corporate World* on the back burner and committed to making his third film. This time he'd be a triple threat—writer, director, and star.

Like many things with Prince, he worked like lightnin'. That was sometimes a good thing. His mind moved at a million miles an hour. Because he was spontaneous and fearless, he got quick results. So many of those results were mind-blowing, others less so. *Graffiti Bridge* was less so.

Prince's plan was simple and, on paper, made sense. Since *Purple Rain* was an unabashed smash, repeat the formula, retool it slightly, and give the people what they wanted. But six years had passed since *Purple Rain* had made its splash. Pop culture had moved on. Pop culture is always moving on. And pop culture, even for someone as savvy as Prince, is slippery as an eel.

*Purple Rain* had an urgency that captured the country. They'd never seen Prince so up close. Never seen him roaring around on a Harley. Never seen his stage shows on the silver screen. He was a new and vital presence. And the plot that he helped cook up—his conflicts with his dad and his rivalry with me—was all he needed.

The second time around, though, the story was stale—what little story there was. His initial idea was to make the movie a vehicle for The Time. He wanted to bring the band back together. Along the way, though, he changed his mind. I'm not sure how long Prince worked on his script, but it felt half baked. He imagined that his father was deceased—though in real life Mr. Nelson was alive and well—and focused mainly on the by-now tired concept of competing with me and my band. I was still "Morris," but now I owned a club called the Pandemonium and was a mafia boss who controlled the city's music scene. In *Purple Rain*, me and my boys were small-time crooks; now we were big-time crooks. Like in *Purple Rain*, Prince was once again the Kid fighting me over the same chick. This time

Aurora replaced Apollonia. I wound up in a garbage heap, Prince wound up with the glamour girl, and the movie wound up disappointing fans and critics alike.

*Come on, man, there were some good scenes.*

Awesome scenes. You had Tevin Campbell singing "Round and Round." You had Mavis Staples singing "Melody Cool." You had funk father George Clinton carrying on. You had Jam, Lewis, Jellybean, Jesse, Monte, and me reunited and kicking it hard. You kicked it hard. The soundtrack was composed of a lot of material you'd been fooling with for years. One new track, "Thieves in the Temple," was a hit. The Time was praised for our work, and we had good jams like "Release It" and "The Latest Fashion," but nothing really jumped off.

Another problem was that, unlike with *Purple Rain*, there were no acting coaches. The look of the picture was stiff because of the limitations of the Paisley sound stage. In trying to bring Hollywood to Minnesota, something got lost along the way. Ralph Waldo Emerson would have applauded Prince for his self-reliance, but Steven Spielberg would hardly be impressed with the back-lot look.

*I didn't notice any hesitancy on the part of u or Jam & Lewis 2 b in the movie.*

There wasn't any. We wanted in. We were banking on the same thing as you—a big box office. Since Jimmy and Terry had missed out on *Purple Rain*, they were especially happy to be in this one. Anyone would be happy to be in a Prince film. But as the scenes were shot, at least for me, the happiness didn't last long. I felt a disconnection. The shit was fragmentary. A lot of it didn't make sense. It wound up being a bunch of musical numbers strung together by a flimsy plot line. I couldn't—and wouldn't—say anything because I was hoping that you'd do your magic and fix all of it in the mix—or in the edit—or maybe in the reshoots. The scenario you set up with *Purple Rain* was repeated with *Graffiti Bridge*. We didn't see the entire film until its premiere. *Purple Rain* warmed my heart. *Graffiti Bridge* left me cold.

Another disappointment that came out of *Graffiti Bridge* . . .

*How long u gonna dwell on disappointments? I don't remember the movie costing u a dime. I remember u got paid.*

Disappointment wasn't with you. It was with me and my reunited band. I liked your idea of us cutting a new album and calling it *Pandemonium*, the name of our nightclub in *Graffiti Bridge*. And I believe that if the film had taken off, the album might have followed suit. It just didn't.

*How 'bout "Jerk Out"?*

Your song and the album's only hit.

*Big hit.*

Number-one smash. A song you'd written before and reworked for us. The video opens with me cackling like a crow. Cut to The Time pulling up to the club in an ultrastretch pink limo convertible. I'm in super MD mode. Half of my vocal was delivered in old school "Rapper's Delight" style, the other half sung as soulfully as the story allowed. The story is basically the same scenario you had been crafting from the get-go: sexual seduction.

A hit is always something to be grateful for—and "Jerk Out" was no different. We were lucky to have a song back on the charts. Monte Moir also brought in a beautiful ballad, "Sometimes I'm Lonely," that I loved singing. As a whole, though, *Pandemonium* never jelled. Maybe because its creation reflected its name. It was cut helter-skelter. We recorded in bits and pieces, sometimes at Paisley, sometimes at Jam and Lewis's Flyte Time studio, sometimes in Hollywood. Prince would pop in and out of the studio. We never knew when. His suggestions were almost always good, but his attention was short-lived. Before we knew it, he'd flown off to destinations unknown.

Can't speak for Jimmy Jam, Terry Lewis, and the other cats, but I think my heart was broken when our reunion didn't result in more than a one-off. I don't want to be too harsh on *Pandemonium* because today, nearly thirty years later, it stands up as sturdy funk. Given the talent playing behind me, it couldn't be anything but good. But a year earlier, when Prince and I started jamming on *Corporate World*, I thought we were back in the rocket ship headed for the moon. This time I thought all our history and energy would come together. Yet in spite of some sparkling songs, after *Pandemonium* it all fell apart.

*4 u. 4 me a lot of positives were set in motion.*

You were always good that way. You were always moving ahead.

*I was already playing with* Diamonds and Pearls.

While The Time was breaking down, you were building up the New Power Generation. (I was pleased you asked me to play drums on the single "New Power Generation." I'd rather play drums behind you than anyone.) You saw the New Power Generation as another way to invent and reenergize. You were going after a younger generation. Even though you were reaching out to new fans, I liked how you used old school–sounding soul sistas like Rosie Gaines. Moving forward, you were also looking back. After *Bad*, Michael got *Dangerous*. You were determined to get even more dangerous. Badder. Bolder.

*U were bold yourself, Morris. Where did that boldness go? What happened 2 u next?*

Glad I finally got you interested in my story.

*Always was, bro. Always will b.*

# 20
# NOTHING IS GUARANTEED

The '90s were rough. I felt like I had lost my identity at roughly the same time Prince lost his.

*I didn't lose mine. I gave mine up.*

Whatever you did, you dropped your name and became a symbol.

*Not a symbol.* THE *symbol.*

When I ran into you out on the road, sometime between your *Love Symbol* album and *Gold Experience*, we were still cool. I remember saying, "Hey, motherfucker, I don't even know what to call you." And you said . . .

*"Don't call me anything."*

So you remember.

*I remember everything.*

I remember being puzzled when I learned about your argument with Warner Brothers. Don't know all the details but I do know they thought you were turning out too much music too soon. They thought you were flooding your own market. I had to laugh. A record company thinking an artist was making too many records. Anyway, when you went out on your own, you made even more records, sold even more records, and proved those motherfuckers wrong. There have been a lot of prolific artists, but when it comes to pure output, Symbol Man puts them all to shame.

While Prince was overproductive, I was worried about being underproductive. I knew that after *Pandemonium* I needed to do another solo record but wasn't sure how to go about it. The Time had timed out. Jimmy Jam and Terry Lewis had recruited Jellybean and Monte Moir to join the Flyte Time team that was turning out massive Janet Jackson hits like *All for You* and *Janet*, her biggest album yet. Everyone around me was having big albums using Minneapolis homeboys. And like everyone in the music business, I was hungry for a hit—a solo hit.

My pal the great bassist Richard "Freeze" Smith helped me put together a girl group we named the Day Zs, formed in the mold of Vanity 6. But the Days Zs never blossomed and the project dried up. Another disappointment.

Then there was this business of my MD image. I was tired of it. That shit was played out. *Graffiti Bridge* had proven that the public was no longer buying into the Prince/Morris rivalry. As always, Prince understood the need for reinvention. And though he dropped his name for a symbol that couldn't be pronounced—the same male-female symbol he formed into his guitar—he saw that such a move would cause even more conversation. Sure, he did it for legal reasons to fuck with Warner Brothers, who still thought he was putting out too much product. And sure, he'd soon start writing "Slave" on his face as a protest of what he considered his unfair recording contract. But Prince was no one's slave and no one's fool. This symbol business was a smart way to expand his brand and boost his sales. He knew no one would ever forget his name. And he was right. During the '90s he became known as "the artist formerly known as Prince." His name remained on the lips of his millions of fans across the globe.

Getting ready for my new solo album, Judi and I moved out of LA to the nearby suburbs. We remodeled a nice five-bedroom ranch-style home in the San Fernando Valley city of Woodland Hills. By then our second son, Derran, was born, another beautiful blessing.

I was loving our family life but not at all loving the kind of record Warner Brothers wanted me to make. They said that musical fashions were changing. Naturally. Musical fashions change like the weather. The label was saying that I needed to change as well. Okay. Change to what?

New Jack Swing was the rage. Michael Jackson had hired New Jack Swing king Teddy Riley to help him create *Dangerous*. So Warner Brothers hired Michael Stokes, a veteran producer who'd worked with Patti LaBelle, because he understood musical fashion. I was a producer myself. I'd been a coproducer with Prince and Jam and Lewis. I'd been produced *by* Prince and Jam and Lewis. In short, I'd been around. I understood that sometimes producers need to be produced. Stokes was also a writer and ace keyboard player. He accepted my input. I cowrote many of the songs and was listed as a coproducer. But I really don't think I earned that title.

The record was called *Guaranteed* and hardly reflected my production or singing style. It was like trying to force a square peg into a round hole. The title tune said I was guaranteed to fix it. But I really wasn't ready to fix anything. One of the songs, "Angel Dope," had a decidedly Bobby Brown New Jack bounce and a rap riff by Big Daddy Kane. Wasn't me. Another song, "Changes," written by me and Stokes, was a soulful ballad more up my alley. I was hoping this might be the hit I was looking for, but my hopes were dashed. *Guaranteed* went nowhere.

The cover of the album was an attempt to soften my image. No more wavy-haired playboy looking to board his private jet. A close-up shot of a more serious cat. But that serious cat's New Jack Swing didn't find favor with the music-buying public. Or with me.

*U r being 2 hard on yourself. Musical talent is musical talent. It don't go away. It just needs the right song 2 bring out that talent. U just didn't have the right song.*

When I listen to *Guaranteed* now, twenty-six years later, I do think I had the right song. "Changes" wasn't even a single but it described what I was going through, both during and after the album's release. With its smooth jazz groove, "Changes" was about a man in transition.

That man was no longer the MD of *Purple Rain*. That man was no longer Morris, leader of The Time. And that man was hardly Morris Day, avatar of a new movement in R&B.

The true avatar remained the man identified by a sexually ambiguous symbol. *Love Symbol* proved to be the Symbol's biggest hit since *Purple Rain*. Prince put together what he called a rock soap opera filled with funk. Right on the heels of that, his *Gold Experience* featured "The Most Beautiful Girl in the World," maybe his most haunting melody, a ballad that went number one. I viewed that with happiness. The '90s belonged to the Symbol. While Michael Jackson was fighting a public relations war he would ultimately lose, the Symbol, even as he fought the mighty music industry, was only gaining strength. I was in awe of that strength.

*The '90s weren't easy 4 me.*

I know that now. I didn't know it then.

*There r some losses that don't need 2 b discussed.*

I heard you, and I respect that. I met your wife Mayte Garcia, but I wasn't around for all that went down. I'll leave that alone.

*Thank u, bro.*

What went down with me was painful enough without speculating about your pain. The short of the matter is that I fucked up.

*How?*

Now you're asking the questions.

*Well, u been so open in this book I figured u wouldn't mind. Besides, this was a time when we were out of touch. I really didn't know what was happenin' with u.*

I wasn't sure what was happenin' myself. I'll try now to break down what was going on inside my head and my heart. My head, I believe, had closed down because my heart was hurt. I'd had three chances to launch a solo career—*Color of Success*, *Daydreaming*, and *Guaranteed*—and all three underperformed. I felt like I'd let myself down.

I also had a shot when I costarred on a sitcom, *Heart and Soul*, with Tisha Campbell. One of the exec producers was Quincy Jones, who was also an exec producer on *The Fresh Prince of Bel-Air*, based on the life of Benny Medina, my A&R man at Warner Brothers. I thought I was in the right place at the right time. I had major Hollywood playas behind me. But *Heart and Soul* didn't last long and my TV career ended before it began.

The good news is that I didn't fall back into drugs. But the bad news is that I fell into another jones. At the time I didn't call it that. I didn't even recognize it as that. But come to find out, sex and love are every bit as seductive a habit as weed and coke.

**That's what I've been saying. Now you're finally hearing me.**

My physical relationship with Judi had lost its charge. Not that I needed an excuse to run off and look for sex in all the wrong places. I can say now what I may not have known then: Maybe I didn't think I was good enough for Judi. Maybe my career disappointments made me feel unworthy to the point where it was hard to face Judi.

Not that Judi put that attitude on me. She knew that navigating the treacherous waters of show business was no easy task. And she wasn't the kind of lady looking to live in a mansion in Malibu. She was cool with our plain suburban crib in Woodland Hills. I was the one with an attitude about myself. I was feeling like a loser. And to lose that feeling—to chase away my blues and escape the reality of a string of failures—I found relief in love. Or what I mistook for love. Find a honey willing to love you all night and you lose all perspective. Find a honey willing to blow your mind sexually and your ego is telling you that you've finally found happiness.

**Yes, sir, that's just what you found. Happiness. Escape.**

Except the escape didn't work for long. All I found was a way to block out the real-life challenges that I eventually had to face: how to be a good husband, how to be a good father, how to keeping pursuing a good career.

So I was blocked. I was so far gone that I paid no attention to business. All my money was flowing out. Nothing was flowing in. Couldn't even afford the house note. We lost the house in Woodland Hills. We lost it all.

Judi had had enough. She put me out. She had already been studying at Pierce College and transferred to UCLA, where she procured graduate housing for adult students. That gave her and our boys a decent place to live in a college environment.

Meanwhile, I found comfort—or discomfort—sleeping on the floor of my big sister's little one-bedroom apartment in Studio City. Sister Sandy had always come to the rescue, but this time the rescue was a lot more complicated than freeing me from substance abuse. I went on the wild with a couple of women who turned out to be as wrong for me as I was wrong for them.

**Maybe wrong but lots of fun.**

The fun didn't last. I was confusing love with lust and lust with love. I was confusing everything. I broke their hearts. They broke mine. I became a broken-down man.

I wish I could report that I used this period away from Judi and our sons as a time for deep self-examination. I wish I could say that I read sacred books and sought out a spiritual mentor. I wish I could tell you that I set up a drum set in my sister's apartment and played night and day, using my musical ability to bang through my depression. I did none of that. I didn't read or listen to music. I didn't seek counseling. I didn't do shit. I slept. I sulked. Morris, the most energetic of men, lost his energy.

*So sorry, bro. U should have reached out.*

Thought of that. Thought of calling you up and saying, "Put me in the studio. Let me cut some tracks. Hire me to do something. Anything." The Temptations said, "Ain't Too Proud to Beg." But I was. Pride's a bitch.

*Don't I know it.*

And me, the man who wrote "A Man's Pride," had too much goddamn pride to admit the truth: I was lost. Going on forty, I felt like I was going on four. A child who just wanted to curl up in bed in the fetal position. Truth is, I did that for longer than I want to admit.

I'd turn on the TV. It was Whitney Houston's time, Mariah Carey's time, Boyz II Men's time, Notorious B.I.G.'s time. All good artists making good music. On Prince's *Gold* album, he had a song that said, "Rock 'n' Roll Is Alive (And It Lives in Minneapolis)." Well, I was only half alive and living at my sister's.

What do I do?

Move back to Minneapolis for inspiration?

I couldn't even consider that. I couldn't even think about being that far away from Judi, Evan, and Derran.

I couldn't think.

I just had to feel.

But feel what?

*The groove. That's what u always felt. The groove is what always brings us back.*

You're right. I had to find the groove.

# 21

# RIGHT TIME FOR THE TIME

It should have been obvious. The Time *was* the groove. The Time had given me life as a musician, and now that my life was falling apart, I had no choice.

"You led a band," said Ron Sweeney, a lawyer/manager who'd worked with some of the biggest act in the '90s. "You can lead that band. You *need* to lead that band again. That band was bigger than you realize. That band is your lifeline."

Ron's call came right on time. An industry powerhouse boosting my deflated self-esteem was exactly what I needed. I required validation. Support. A cheerleader.

For all the months I was hibernating at my sister's, I did go over to UCLA to visit Judi and our sons. Judi was doing great, majoring in history and preparing for prelaw. She was holding down the fort as a single mom. She never locked me out. Never used the kids to get back at me. In fact, Judi eventually forgave me. I needed forgiveness to break through my depression.

Depression is a baffling disease that baffles the smartest shrinks. I had it. My antidepressant medication had been acting out with chicks. When I stopped taking that medication, I had to face facts:

Acting out with chicks would never get me what I wanted. I wanted my life back.

To take me back, Judi had a proviso: Stay on my music game and go to counseling.

Staying on my music game was easy but counseling wasn't. Don't matter if the counselor is a man or a woman. I'm never comfortable in that situation.

*Well, u r writing all kinds of intimate stuff in a book 2 a bunch of readers u don't know. They r strangers, & u r spilling your guts 2 them. Y not 2 a counselor?*

Writing this book, I'm alone in a room. Besides, writing isn't talking. I write in silence. That's why I dig it. But I didn't dig revealing the most private feelings to someone charging two hundred bucks an hour. Maybe I'm wrong, but I can't see you as the kind of cat who liked counseling any more than me.

*This is your book, not mine.*

You and I came from the same place. We weren't brought up to open up to shrinks.

*Can't argue with u.*

I tried arguing with Judi. Said that I already knew I'd fucked up and didn't really need to go over my fuck-ups. But Judi wanted some reassurances. She felt that those fuck-ups had torn us apart and needed to be looked at. So I caved in and went into couples therapy.

I'd have to say that it worked 'cause we got back together. But I'd also have to say that in those sessions I was always inferior to Judi. That hardly made me feel good. In these therapy sessions she always shone and, at least in my mind, I always retreated. I was a fish out of water.

No matter—the fish survived and started swimming.

Ron Sweeney tested the market and learned that there was a still a demand for The Time. He lined up dates. Now I had to line up a band. Jellybean and Monte, who had been working with Jam and Lewis, were ready to come on board. They wanted to get back out on the road and kick ass. Freeze was down. He'd be our bass man. William Bryant, who'd played with Marvin Gaye, was on keys. And Tori Ruffin, who burned on guitar, also signed on.

Those first rehearsals did more to diffuse depression than a boatload of Prozac. When Jellybean kicked off the jam, I felt instant relief. Instant transformation. Can't say enough about my man Jellybean. In the long history of the entangled maze of American music—blues, gospel, folk, soul, pop, rock, you name it—there have been dozens, maybe hundreds, of killer drummers. Some, like Sonny Payne, possessed the power to fuel big bands. Others, like Kenny Clarke, had new and nuanced visions of timekeeping. All of them speak to me. As a drummer myself, all of them have taught me. But for all the amazing skill, say, of Keith Moon, John Bonham, or Billy Cobham, give me Jellybean Johnson every time. Give me Jellybean when I want to feel the funk in my gut. Give me Jellybean when I need to bring my tired ass back to life. Garry George "Jellybean" Johnson breathes beats like normal folk breathe air. We might be rehearing for five straight hours, but I'll be damned if Jellybean, right after rehearsal, doesn't go out to a club where he can sit in with another band and keep tearing it up till the break of dawn.

Monte Moir is also a motherfucker, a musician/writer/singer/arranger who's never gotten his proper due. He was born white but plays black as the ace of spades. Monte's a magician on keys. Same's true of Freeze on bass. All these cats aren't just good; they're great. But it was their goodness and devotion to me—and to the idea of a band greater than the sum of its parts—that lifted the fog and brought me back into the world of commerce and creativity. I realized that The Time was a living force that, once unleashed, could blast its way through whatever storms might be out there. The Time was beyond tenacious, beyond strong. The Time was even beyond time.

*I hear u. Maybe that's y, just like u, I could never give up on The Time.*

The Time was what brought us back together. But like everything in our lives, that was complicated. The Time had torn us apart in the past, and The Time almost tore us apart in the future.

*I didn't c it that way. Besides, I just said something nice. Y introduce a negative into my positive?*

Difficulties ain't necessarily negative. They're just obstacles. But whatever they are, they're real. A real part of our story.

*If u gotta tell it, u gotta tell it.*

I will. But not now. Now it's 1997. Now it's a sunny morning in the peaceful town of Roswell, twenty-two miles north of Atlanta. Judi, Evan, Derran, and I have been living in Georgia for a couple years. After living in a three-bedroom apartment we've moved into a home on Wild Greene Drive. I'm no longer struggling with my wild side. The reincarnation of The Time has proven successful. We're back in the money—not crazy money but good money, good enough to let us lead a quiet suburban life. Clean streets. Manicured lawns. Kicked-back vibe.

Judi and I get up early. We slip into our running gear and head out to a nearby woodsy path. We're both joggers and dig jogging side by side. We maintain the same pace. We're finally in sync.

Back home, we have our coffee and a light breakfast and get to work. Calling myself "Eugene Knight," I call promoters to book the band.

Judi finished up at UCLA. She passed the LSAT exam in preparation for law school when her entrepreneurial energy took another turn. She'd been making superdelicious butter toffee for friends and family at Christmas. Now she's being encouraged to actually start a candy business. She gears up quickly and soon is marketing exclusively at trade shows.

Life is busy.

The Time Nation—if I can call it that—was larger than any of us had imagined. The Time Nation is also expanding. And all without a new record. The strength of the old hits, together with our association with Prince . . .

*Thank u . . .*

. . . is filling nightclubs, concert halls, and even small arenas. I'm finally comfortable with who I am. Jerome still brings out the mirror, and the audience still loves it, but the focus is on the funk. MD is finally Morris, not a character in a movie but the leader of a band that has managed to resurrect the very thing that got us going back in high school: grooves to crush you. Those original raw Minneapolis grooves that, if anything, have grown nastier over time.

So far so good. And then things get better. Judi becomes pregnant and Cameron, our third son, is born on November 1, 1999.

We're cruising into the new millennium time. Everything's on the upswing. Everything's cool. Morris Day and The Time even get an on-screen appearance to close out a big-budget Hollywood comedy, *Jay and Silent Bob Strike Back*, featuring Chris Rock, Will Ferrell, and Ben Affleck.

In the midst of all the fun, here comes a phone call. You can guess who was on the other end of the line.

*They don't have 2 guess. They already know.*

Tell 'em anyway.

*Me.*

# 22

# RAVES AND RANTS

*Actually it wasn't me. I don't like using the phone.*

But it was someone speaking for you. Same thing. And the big thing was that you were inviting The Time back into Prince World.

*I wouldn't go that far. I was planning a show.*

And wanted us on it.

*True. I figured that Morris Day had paid the dues 2 tell the news.*

And we were ready. Whoever called me made it sound like it was gonna be the biggest event since the Big Bang.

*Should have called it the Big Bang.*

Instead you gave a typical Prince-sounding handle—RaveUn2 the Year 2000. Hyped-up to the max.

*How u gonna call it hype when it was the end of a century & the start of a new millennium?*

You found a way. You were set on exploiting "1999," a song you'd written seventeen years before. It was a great party song but a strange one—strange 'cause even though you wanna party like it's 1999, you also talk about the date to come—New Year's Eve 2000—as judgment day. The sky's turning purple and people are running from war and destruction. Sounds like the apocalypse. Is that what you were predicting back then?

*Your interpretation, not mine.*

What's yours?

*Said it b4. Will say it again. I don't interpret.*

Whatever you had in mind for that New Year's Eve, you did it up big time. Weeks before December 31, you had The Time come play Paisley. You were there.

*U really thought I'd stay away?*

I didn't know. But when you showed up, we couldn't have been happier. We took up where we left off. Didn't miss a beat.

During rehearsals your man said you wanted me swinging out into the audience on a rope. Fuck that shit. All my swinging would be restricted to music. When I refused, they found a stuntman to act as my double.

*I was disappointed. I wanted 2 c u fly, bro.*

I bet you did. But I was staying on the ground. That was the night we put on the show of shows. Can't remember kicking it any harder. After all those years we wanted to prove to you that we still had it.

*U did.*

Then you produced another show, this time with Lenny Kravitz, George Clinton, Maceo Parker, and Rosie Gaines, your "Diamonds and Pearls" girl. You also reunited some of the Sly and the Family Stone band—Cynthia Robinson, Jerry Martini, and Larry Graham. Larry had been with you for a while. I think by then he'd started talkin' to you 'bout Jehovah's Witnesses.

Anyway, you were looking to put these two concerts together for a live video. I was a little shocked at how, before breaking into "Purple Rain," you fell into some heavy preaching.

*That bother u?*

It was different. Different part of you coming out. Thought I knew you really well but then I saw something I hadn't seen before. Before, you loved talking street like the rest of us. Salty language was part of our stew. But you said you'd stop cursing. Then a little later you said you wanted to go back and remove the sexy references from all your songs. Well, if you did that, there'd be hardly anything left.

All this left us confused. Then you dropped the symbol and became Prince again. I wondered whether the symbol, which had a lot to do with sex . . .

*Says u . . .*

Says anyone who looks at it. I wondered whether the symbol maybe represented your ego and your ego was something you wanted to surrender to God. How, though, does an entertainer/genius like you abandon your ego, the same ego that's been driving you since day one to become the biggest artist on the planet?

In giving up the symbol and reclaiming the royal name, I didn't see you giving up the customized guitar shaped into the symbol. You'd be playing that guitar and wearing that symbol as a pendant around your neck for years to come. Personally, I dug it. Years earlier you said that the symbol came to you in a meditation. I believed you. It was a righteous representation. I also believe that certain artists, no matter how deep their religious convictions, are so downright sexual that sex can never be drained from their art. And that's fine. That's you. The sexual ambiguity, the male and female commingling, was there from the start. It *was* your start. In those early days you took a lot from your hairdressers and their feminine ways. You looked to fool around with your feminine side, and that's cool. Then you had your macho side. Cool too. But it was the combination of the two that made you. Made you different. And got you the attention you wanted.

*I ain't commenting.*

You don't got to. There are thousands of images of you out there in the world—images that you created and generated—that prove my point.

At the end of the century, Prince was changing and Prince was not changing. He was the same guy I'd always known, but also different. Something was shifting. I wanted to be sensitive to that shift but didn't know how to go about it. So I chilled. I just listened. For example:

During that same weekend The Time played Paisley Park for the Rave thing, he had The Time meet him in one of his studios. We were hoping we might get to record with him. But no. He wanted to have a talk with us. Before that, I'd never known Prince to have talks. It had always been about rehearsing, playing, and perfecting music. Prior to the talk, we were told that while at Paisley we couldn't eat any form of meat or drink any kind of booze.

Prince's talk was long. And boring. He wasn't talking with us; he was talking *at* us. He was preaching. Essentially he was telling us to embrace the Jehovah's Witness system of belief. He was using all sorts of arguments—that was the boring part—to prove his point.

Being no Bible scholar, I didn't argue with anything he said. Didn't argue because I knew that the one part of Prince's personality that had not changed was his need to control everyone and everything around him. Including others' religious beliefs. You can't go up against that control. You just gotta let it slide over you, which was what I did.

In my silence, though, I was thinking that his beliefs made no sense. In my simpleminded way, I saw the two books of the Bible, the Old and New Testaments, as anything but simple. Many, many passages are hard to understand. They require interpretation, and they can be interpreted a million ways. Prince said no. Only one way to interpret these books. All other interpretations are wrong. But to prove his interpretation he had to set out an incredibly complicated system. A convoluted system. But even if I followed that system, I couldn't get with its conclusion: that when Jesus comes back he's only going to bring to Glory those who have embraced this system. The rest of us are going to hell in a handbasket.

Makes no sense. If Jesus is the God of love, this ain't no loving act. If Jesus is the God of inclusion, this ain't no inclusive act. If Jesus is the God of forgiveness, this don't look like forgiveness to me. It's harsh. It makes Jesus out to be a strict and even cruel high school principal, not the merciful and compassionate soul who came to save the world—all the world—through the power of sweet love.

Prince preached with very little sweetness. He was arrogant. He was insistent. Part of me wanted to stand up and voice my objections, but I knew better. Prince could outtalk me. Prince could outsmart me. And Prince also had the power to hire or not hire my band again. The cool move was to make no move at all. Just sit and listen and hope the endless rant would end soon.

The rant was so long that it came in two parts. Prince gave us a short break. He probably had to use the facilities. While he was gone, my guitarist, Tori, who knew I had a flask of cognac on me, asked for a taste.

**And you said you weren't getting high no more. But this cognac felt good, didn't it? Real fuckin' good.**

The cognac was no big deal. Just a little sip now and then. Anyway, I passed Tori the flask. Then Prince reappeared and restarted the sermon. More tortuous proof of why the holy books point to one conclusion and one conclusion only. When Prince reached the climax of his argument, the cognac flask slipped out of the pocket of Tori's oversized jeans onto the floor. Everyone, including Prince, just stared at it. Without saying a word, Tori picked up the flask and put it back in his pocket while Prince resumed his attempt to convert The Time.

Fortunately there was no altar call. Had there been, not a single one of us would have answered the call. Instead Prince offered a final prayer, asking that we might receive the truth as the truth had been revealed to him by God Almighty.

After Prince left the room, we sat there for a few seconds, shaking our heads in disbelief. In the hours that followed, I kept thinking about this change in him. I could dig it in this sense: Prince didn't like confusion. Religion can be confusing. And confusion can be scary. Prince liked answers. He liked clarity. He liked feeling secure. Big Chick made him feel secure. His music had always made him feel secure. Now he wanted to feel secure about his spiritual beliefs. Jehovah's Witnesses gave him that feeling of security. It wiped out confusion. It gave him the assurance that when it came to matters of faith, he was absolutely, incontrovertibly right.

*More of your dime-store psychology.*

Psychology that fits you to a T, my brotha.

*4 someone who doesn't like my sermonizing, u don't seem 2 mind doing a whole lot of sermonizing of your own.*

Not telling anyone what to think. Just saying what *I* think. I know that God has chosen to stay invisible. And also inaudible. I also know that Jesus chose not to write a single word. To me, all that means is that God has decided to wrap himself up in a cloak of silence. We can't see him, we can't hear him, and we can't read any words that he himself wrote. So it's only reasonable to have some doubts about stuff in the Bible. Or, as Gershwin wrote, "It Ain't Necessarily So." Yet without doubts, there's no faith. Faith is built on doubt.

Another weird thing: As an adult, Prince adopted the religion that his archrival Michael Jackson had adopted as a child. Michael's mom, Katherine, had become a Jehovah's Witness and Michael went along with her beliefs. He kept those beliefs until 1987, when he was twenty-nine years old. Prince adopted those beliefs when he was around thirty-nine. Don't know what to make of that except to say that it's strange. Two towering musical geniuses leaving and entering a superstrict religious cult at different times. You can't get away from the Michael/Prince comparisons. The analogies are haunting.

I also believe Prince was always haunted by his dad.

*Do we got 2 go there?*

Look, I didn't really know my dad well enough to be haunted by him. We didn't have a real relationship. At least you had a dad who was present in your life. In your growing-up years, your dad was a big deal. I know you wanted him to be proud of you, and he was. His DNA was rich with music. You took that music all over the world. Not to criticize him, but he never took his music anywhere outside Minneapolis. He got off on all you accomplished. I believe you were grateful. He gave you great musical genes.

*Sure, I was grateful.*

I remember when you gave him one of your houses.

*& he was grateful 4 that.*

All good. But there's only one thing I never understood.

*What's that?*

When he died in 2001—I believe he was eighty-five—he was still living in that house.

*He was.*

And I know that the death of a dad is always rough, even one who's lived a long life.

*What's your point?*

Just weeks after his death, you bulldozed that house to the ground. Why would you go and do that?

*Y not?*

Seems strange.

*2 u. Not 2 me.*

You had a habit of bulldozing old houses you no longer needed. I never understood why.

*U don't have 2 understand. I was clearing ground.*

To lay a new foundation?

*Said I don't need 2 explain. Y don't u just go on with your story. Get back 2 the music. Folks wanna read about the music.*

# 23

# IT'S ABOUT TIME

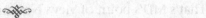

By 2003, my marriage wasn't in the best shape.

**That's 'cause I was back.**

Not the reason. I wasn't doing drugs.

**You were jonesing on women. Same thing. You were hooked.**

I don't think so.

**Ask Judi about that.**

Judi thought I was addicted to everything, but she didn't understand. Her thing was counseling, counseling, counseling. I went along 'cause I wanted to save my family. But I didn't like it. What did I need to be counseled about?

**My point exactly. Just go on out there and party as much as you can. Get loose. Get down. Get it all.**

Wasn't like that. Judi's a great lady, but our physical thing had lost its allure. Physical is important to me. Real important. It was almost like she'd become my business partner, or my sister, or even my mother. The whole thing was making me uncomfortable, especially her uncompromising demands that we continue couples therapy, where I just clammed up.

**And clammed me up too. I could have said all kinds of shit about wanting to get high on something. Sex might not be coke, but it's a surefire high.**

That's MD's point of view. Not mine.

**You sure 'bout that?**

I'm sure I was focused on my career. One night, for instance, we were playing the House of Blues on Sunset in LA. Killing it. After the first set, someone handed me a note.

"Nelly's manager wants to meet you."

Nelly was the hottest rapper out there. Coincidentally, I'd recently heard him mention me during a TV interview. "I like Morris Day," he said. "I've always liked his beats. But wondering where he's hanging out these days."

His manager, Courtney Benson, said the same thing: "We're all Morris fans."

**I see you trippin'.**

Not trippin', just enjoying a few kind words. It's pleasin'—and natural to be pleased—to know you're appreciated.

Courtney wanted to know if I had a record deal. I didn't.

"I can get you one," he said.

"If I had a dollar for every dude who said he could get me a record deal, I'd be rich enough not to need one."

"Well, I'm not every dude," said Courtney. "I'm a dude who does what he says."

And he did. After being turned down by a bunch of labels, Courtney got the bright idea of going to Bob Cavallo, former Prince manager and one of the *Purple Rain* producers, who'd switched tracks to head up Disney's Hollywood Records.

"Morris in good shape?" Bob asked Courtney.

"Great shape."

Bob flew me in from Atlanta, saw I was sharp as a tack and clean as the board of health—

**That you speakin' or me?**

Me being objective. Bob saw that I was a working artist who'd rediscovered his groove. Sensing I was ready to cut some fresh funk, he put a decent deal on the table. Courtney had come through. Tenacious and talented, Courtney would faithfully serve as my manager from then till now. My brother, Jesse, who'd take a bullet for me, had become our skillful road manager, learning all the tricks of the trade. My team was in place.

I had to call my debut Hollywood release *It's About Time*. Because it was. We revisited The Time's old hits and added four originals that I cowrote. Worked with a couple of hip hip-hoppers. Jazze Pha was one, but logistics kept us from releasing his contribution. E-40 rapped on "In My Ride," a single that made some noise.

The record got good play. The label threw a release party where The Time was slated to play the new joints live at the Malibu Inn. Prince showed up. Always glad to see Prince. There was no pushback from when we hadn't responded to his preaching back at Paisley. We were cool.

He didn't sit in, and I'm not sure he stayed for our whole set, but later I learned he approached one of the Hollywood Records execs and said, "Y'all better promote this new record right. These are my boys."

After everything that had come down, he still saw The Time as his. I didn't mind at all.

I did mind, though, when I learned through his camp that once he heard the finished record he wasn't really feeling it. But Takumi Suetsugu, Prince's longtime guitar tech, kept touting it. He praised it so strong that the boss took another listen and—this is a big deal for Prince—actually called me.

"It's nice," was all he said.

That was all I needed to hear.

To reinforce his support, he reached out to me when The Time was in New York promoting *It's About Time* on *Good Morning America*.

He'd rented out a club where he was having a private party. He wanted me there.

When I arrived, I saw Prince deejaying in the booth. He was spinnin' all his favorite joints, Marvin's "Got to Give It Up," James's "Popcorn," Sly's "I Want to Take You Higher." He was a kid in the candy store. At one point he gave the deejay duties over to Q-Tip. Chillin' in the club were Queen Latifah, Lenny Kravitz, Fred Wesley—every sort of musical luminary you can imagine.

"Got something new in mind," he told me that night.

"What is it?" I asked.

"When the time is right," he said, "you'll know about it. The whole world's gonna know about it."

"Got a name for it?"

"Not yet . . . but soon."

# 24

# MUSICOLOGY

Gonna quote an old-school hipster friend who chooses to stay anonymous:

"In the '50s, I saw Chuck Berry, Little Richard, and Bo Diddley live. I saw Ray Charles and his small band play a small club in Dallas. In Fayetteville, Arkansas, in the '60s, I watched Ike and Tina practically burn down a barroom. When I saw the Stax reviews—with Otis Redding and Sam and Dave—and the Motown reviews—with Junior Walker and Stevie Wonder—I couldn't imagine being more moved until the '70s came around, when I caught Al Green in Memphis and Teddy Pendergrass in Philly. In the '80s, Michael Jackson's Bad Tour took my breath away. In the '90s, Janet Jackson and Whitney Houston performed magnificently. But as great as these shows were—and believe me, they were spectacular—the single greatest display of raw soul talent I've ever witnessed was when, in 2004, Maceo Parker marched onstage in a cap and gown to kick off Prince's miraculous set of his Musicology Tour."

The Time was on that tour. Here's the backstory.

We were doing *The Late Show*. Jay Leno was a fan. During rehearsals I looked up and saw Prince sitting in the first row.

"Y'all sound good," he said. "Ever think of working with Lil Jon?"

Lil Jon was a hot rapper/producer/writer.

"No," I said. "Why you asking?"

"He's got the right feel for The Time," said Prince. "He feels your flavor and he's got flavors of his own."

I appreciated Prince's advice. The Lil Jon hookup never happened, but I liked how Prince was always looking for new ways to accessorize The Time.

"That new jam I was telling you about in New York is finally together," he added. "Whole new concept. Musicology. Bringing back old-school funk with a new attitude."

"Isn't that what we've always tried to do?"

"But now I'm doing it with more fire. Tired of these machines. Tired of this computer-making music. I'm talkin' 'bout strong and solid and in-your-face. I want y'all on the tour."

"Cool."

"Look at the schedule."

Prince handed me a piece of paper. Looked like he was hitting at least forty venues. I got excited, not only for getting back with the man but for the payday. I figured the bread had to be big. The future was suddenly brighter than ever.

Little while later Prince showed up during The Time show at Studio 54 in Vegas. It was another one of those moments when he felt moved to jump onstage, grab a bass or guitar—can't remember which—and funk along with us. We played seamlessly together. Old times. Good times. Because he had formed The Time, he could slip in and out of it with perfect precision. Add to that his nostalgic frame of mind. In 2004, we took him back thirty years to when he was just finessing his funk.

Afterward, he was still talkin' big about *Musicology*, calling it the bomb. In promoting the Musicology Tour his mantra was "Bring back the real music." He was making war on coldhearted machines. In hindsight, we see that he lost that war. Maybe, though, the battle isn't over yet. Maybe we still need to heed Prince's charge for real musicians playing real instruments.

The heart of *Musicology* is the title song and the moving autobiographical video. Prince channels a sparsely slick classic groove, softening it a bit even as he tightens the screws. It's all about lighting up an old-school joint for what Prince calls the true funk soldiers.

The video opens on Prince as a little boy riding his bike to the Counterpoint Book and Record Store. Counter to what's happening in music in 2004, Prince is pointing to the past. The past is the '60s. The store proprietor is reading a *Cashbox* with a young Marvin Gaye on the cover. Posters of Ray Charles, the Drifters, and Major Lance are all over the store. Little Prince buys a ticket for the Prince Musicology show that comes with a free copy of a 45 rpm single of the song itself. All for a buck. The boy goes home. The walls of his bedroom are covered with photos of Jimi Hendrix and Sly Stone. He immediately drops the needle on "Musicology," picks out the groove on his guitar and uses Mom's upright vacuum cleaner as a mic as he breaks into dance. From Little Prince we switch to Big Prince in concert, singing a song that calls out Earth, Wind & Fire, Sly, Chuck D, and, of course, James Brown, the godfather and chief inspiration of this ancient newfangled funk. In the end, Little Prince arrives at the concert, where, at the climax of the jam, Big Prince, wearing a polka-dotted neckband, throws his matching polka-dotted pocket square out into the crowd. Little Prince grabs it and suddenly the two are matched up. The two are one. Little Prince, Big Prince, One Prince. The adult hugs his inner child. It's sweet enough to make a grown man like me cry.

The tour itself almost made me cry for different reasons.

Prince sensed all this new energy from The Time. He made it clear we were part of the bottom-line basics of *Musicology*. He was promoting live old-school R&B and by then we were in the forefront of old-school funk. He gave us the idea we were in for the long run. As it turned out, his idea changed.

*How's that?*

You didn't come through. Weren't true to your word.

*Y not?*

We never got a contract that said we were opening every show of what was officially called the Musicology Live 2004ever Tour. Your tune changed when all your people said was that we'd be playing on "many dates." What happened to "all the dates"?

*R u saying that* Musicology *didn't help reexpose u 2 the Prince fan base?*

Helped us plenty. And helped you plenty as well. We'd open for you in a major market and tear half the roof off the arena until you came out and tore off the other half. It was incredible. But then you'd drop us for a week or two or three. If ticket sales slowed down, rumors would go out—"The Time is gonna be the opening act." That would boost sales. You'd give us another couple of shows only to drop us again. That happened all summer long.

Some people said it happened 'cause you felt too much heat from our playing. I don't believe that. I think you were just being your usual whimsical, unpredictable self.

On those shows that we did open, I was not surprised to see no deterioration in your focus. For an 8 p.m. show, you arrived at the venue by noon. Even after sound check, you spent hours zipping around in a golf cart, testing the acoustics from every possible angle. You wore a wireless mic and gave instructions to the engineers. The prep routines before your shows were like military drills. Your precision was awe-inspiring. I know we rose to the occasion and met your standards because you never said a negative word. At the same time, I couldn't get you to commit to a schedule. You were playing with me the way you always like to play. It was frustrating but also exhilarating. We took whatever you gave us.

*I didn't hear any complaints.*

Even if I had wanted to complain, there was no way. You claimed not to carry a cell phone. Or if you did, I didn't have the number. Despite our long history and strong friendship, I couldn't drop by your dressing room for a one-on-one. Between you and me were massive walls of security, protective assistants, and stern managers.

After the tour ended, I was feeling ambivalent. On one hand, great: We'd never sounded better; you'd never sounded better. On the other hand, not so great: We could have worked ten times as many dates as we were given.

Maybe it was because I didn't complain that I got a call from one of those stern managers to come to Paisley Park. Prince was in his post-touring mode. That meant he was back in the studio cutting new tracks. There was some stuff he wanted me to hear.

My patience had paid off. I landed in Minneapolis and hopped right over to Paisley. This time no waiting, no games. Go directly to the studio. Prince was waiting. Prince was smiling when I arrived. Big hug. Big compliments on all the good Time reviews from the Musicology Tour. He said The Time had been in his head and he had written some tracks with us in mind. Did that mean he wanted to hook up with us again? Did he want to sign us? Produce us? Those questions were pressing, but I knew better than to ask. Just let the funk fly. Let me hear the tracks.

I loved them. They were hits. They were raw and needed work, but that made them even better. That meant Prince wanted me to help him finish them. We were back in business.

Or were we?

# 25

# THE COME-TO-JESUS TALK

Prince and I had been working in the studio for over a week. We were making beats, singing, working up these tracks into songs. He was inspiring me, and I don't think it's just my ego saying that I inspired him. We got off on each other's energy and ideas. I was also especially hopeful because, even though he was clearly in charge, it was less about control and more about collaboration. Maybe because I had once left his camp over the issue of creative control, this time around he seemed less interested in asserting control. It almost seemed like he wanted to placate me. I took that to mean he respected the fact that I had gone off on my own and over the decades had made Morris Day and The Time a sustainable band. I'd honored the music that was a vital part of his legacy.

We got to the point where we had six songs and were ready to record. Prince wanted these for a new Time album that he and I would coproduce. Once we cut these, the plan was to complete the project by writing four more songs. He talked about The Time opening on his next tour, not intermittently like on Musicology but every night. Guaranteed. We'd call in the lawyers and put it on paper.

Before that, though, he said he wanted to have a talk.

What about?

Spirituality.

What about spirituality?

He said he didn't want to go forward unless we were on the same spiritual page.

Exactly what does that mean?

Everything he'd been talking about.

Did that mean he wanted me to officially sign up as a Witness?

Yes.

Well, I wasn't ready to do that.

Why not?

It's personal. It's nothing to argue about.

He said I was saying that because I couldn't win the argument.

I said he was probably right but I still didn't want to argue.

Me either, he said. I just want you to accept the Truth.

Maybe there's more than one truth, I said.

Wrong. There is only one truth. And I want you to know it.

Why is that so important to you? I asked.

Because you're part of me. You've always been part of me.

When Prince said that, I was touched. I was moved.

You're my brother, he added. I want you to know God.

But I feel like I already know God.

But to truly know him you have to know his teachings.

Is it really that complicated?

I can break it down for you.

No, thanks.

Why the resistance? he asked.

Why the insistence? I asked back.

Think about it, he urged.

I will, I said.

In truth, there was nothing to think about. As much as I wanted to cowrite and coproduce with Prince, as much as I wanted back in his good graces and back in his world of huge stadium shows and massive international exposure, how could I say I believed in something that I didn't? The last thing in the world I wanted to do was go knocking on doors to convert strangers to something I saw as bizarre.

It wasn't a close call. I wasn't about to become a Witness to boost my career. Besides, whether I'm right or not, it felt like a cult. And I'm about the last person who'd ever join a cult.

I didn't tell him no right then and there because I didn't want to be disrespectful. But the more I thought about it, the stranger it seemed. No matter how deeply you adhere to a religion, do you really want to say that unless your colleague embraces that religion he'll no longer be your colleague?

The whole thing brought me down. Just when I thought Prince was getting less controlling in the studio, he was getting more controlling in an area where he had no business being controlling at all. Made me mad. I figured the best way to handle it, though, was to keep the anger to myself. I went back to give him a second chance. The next day we had a second talk. This one much shorter.

I wanted to know if he was sure this was how he wanted to handle it.

He was sure.

Was he sure he wanted to mix up music and religion?

He didn't see it as a mix-up. He saw it as all one thing.

But he wasn't going to put religious lyrics on these songs, was he?

No. But that didn't matter. Was I in his camp or wasn't I?

I wasn't.

I couldn't.

I didn't.

I split.

I never expected to hear from him about those songs again, and I never did. For all I know, they're somewhere in his vast vault of unreleased material.

*U make it sound like I deserted u. I never did.*

Didn't say you did. But I am saying that some years passed before I got an invitation to your crib in Bel Air.

*&, if memory serves right, u came running.*

Who wouldn't? By then the Kid had conquered Hollywood.

**And we wanted in on the action, didn't we?**

Who's this "we?"

**The Morris and MD team looking to get what we could.**

Wasn't like that. Prince was the last person on the planet to have any drug parties.

**But the ladies!**

I looked. Everyone looks. But there's a world of difference between looking and lurking. Besides, it wasn't 'bout the ladies either. It was about music. Prince asked The Time to come up and play at one of his famous private parties. I was glad and also surprised. I thought my refusal to become a Witness had permanently put me in the penalty box. So I was relieved to learn that Prince had let bygones be bygones.

This was the famous palatial pad he was renting for $95,000 a month from NBA hooper Carlos Boozer. The address got famous when he named an album after it: 3121. (Later he also packaged and promoted a 3121 perfume.) Wasn't enough that my boy leased the place; he went on and purple-ized it. The gates opened to a purple driveway that led to a purple-carpeted grand entryway into the estate, where all the floors were purple and all the rooms had oversized portraits of Prince. Before we played, Prince gave me the tour. Twelve bedrooms. A hair salon. A massage parlor. And, in the place of Boozer's big gym, Prince had put a purple-themed nightclub complete with a deejay booth. That's where The Time got to play to Prince's dazzling array of Hollywood stars.

Another time he asked me and Courtney to drop by 3121 as guests. The party people were already partying. Walking toward the gym turned nightclub, I heard "Superstitious." I wondered whether it was a record or Stevie. It was Stevie. For the next song, Prince motioned for me to get on the drums but when he saw that Questlove had already started breaking out some beats, he put me on keyboard. Still directing—always directing—Prince had Anthony Hamilton and Erykah Badu singing background. We sang old-school stuff—Motown,

Gamble and Huff, '80s funk, '90s funk—you name it, Prince singing lead, then Stevie, then me. There were fountains of chocolate syrup where everyone was dipping strawberries, everyone dancing, chatting it up, having themselves a good ol' time. It was crazy. Crazy good. And then it looked like it was gonna get even better.

After one of those 3121 shindigs, Prince came up to me. Usually when he wanted to do business with me, he did it through his people. But this time he wanted to do it himself. I wondered why.

*Cause I had a gig that I knew would make u happy. A big gig. A milestone gig. A hometown gig.*

A gig I'd rather forget.

*U will have 2 say y.*

I will.

# 26

# THE GIG THAT WASN'T

Prince was a numbers man. Ever since he wrote 1999 in the '80s he'd liked fooling with numbers. I remember him telling me that 7 is one of the holiest numbers because it signifies spiritual perfection. I think that's one of the reasons that he chose 7/7/7 for his Minneapolis extravaganza. Like all Prince events, he was going for broke. He pointed out that this would be his first concert at the downtown Target Center arena since 1999. In addition to the show that night, he was making an appearance at Macy's to introduce his 3121 fragrance.

I didn't know anything about this until one of Prince's managers called to say that he wanted The Time on the show. Was I willing?

Yes. I was a little surprised at the offer. He could have picked any band, but choosing us warmed my heart. The bond still couldn't be broken. Making things even more exciting was his announcement of an aftershow at First Avenue, scene of *Purple Rain*.

"He wants this reunion to be really special," his man told me, "and he wants you guys to be a big part of it."

Cool.

After we negotiated a good fee that stipulated I'd have to pay for my band's transportation, the schedule arrived. There would be rehearsals and sound checks at both the arena and the club. We were told where we'd be staying. I'd never heard of the place. It was a motel thirty miles from downtown in the vicinity of Paisley. Why would we be staying out there when the shows were downtown? There were a dozen good hotels downtown. I asked his man to explain. He couldn't. I asked him to reserve a hotel downtown. He wouldn't. He said the instructions had come directly from Prince.

When we arrived at the motel and saw it was a dump I said, "We're moving." And we did. We checked into a nice hotel near the Target Center. But forget this hotel stuff. All that mattered was the music. The big show at the Target. The aftershow at First Avenue. Getting to play live with Prince. The beautiful feeling of coming home to where it all began.

And then the hammer came down.

"You're canceled," said Prince's man.

This was two nights before 7/7/7.

"What do you mean canceled?"

"Prince doesn't want you on the show."

"Why?"

"Don't know."

"We at least deserve to know why."

"Call Prince."

"I don't have his phone number."

"He doesn't have a phone."

"Then how can I ask him why he's canceling us?"

"I don't know. Besides, it doesn't make any difference."

"What about getting paid?"

"We're not paying because you're not playing."

"I paid five thousand dollars just to fly my guys here."

"Not my problem. Gotta run."

Click.

I was beyond pissed. If I had a way to get to Prince, I would have. But I knew, especially with him making personal appearances and playing these shows, his security would be beefed up. I'd never reach him. And maybe that was for the better. Because if I had, I would have said shit that I'd later regret.

Motherfucker. You book us for a gig—not just any gig but a heart-warming homecoming gig—and then, without explanation, you kick our ass to the curb. That ain't right.

When I got back to Atlanta, I had my management give Prince's people holy hell. They never would agree to pay our performance fee, but at least they coughed up the $5,000 for transportation.

It all left a sour taste in my mouth, especially because Prince never bothered to call and explain why he'd kicked us off the show. Was he still pissed that I hadn't become a Witness? Had someone actually bothered to tell him that we had changed hotels and that somehow had bothered him? I didn't know. I'll never know. Nine years passed before I saw Prince again.

But flying out of the Minneapolis–St. Paul International Airport, there was something else on my mind a lot more powerful than my drama with Prince.

I had just become a father for the sixth time. My son Elijah had been born earlier that July. As with the birth of all my children, I was grateful for his safe delivery and presence in my life.

There was only one complication. His mother was not my wife, Judi. His mother was Lorena. I had fallen head-over-heels in love with Lorena.

To explain my anguish won't be easy. I say that because Judi had done nothing to justify my betrayal of our bond. And Lorena had done nothing to lure me away from my marriage.

It was all my doing, and it was a mess.

# 27

# GIGOLOS GET LONELY TOO

*Now I'm getting 2 learn about stuff I never heard.*

Hard to write about romance.

*I never did.*

Except in song.

*But like I said b4, a song doesn't need an explanation.*

And I feel like I do need to explain. Explain to Judi. Explain to Lorena. Explain to my children. Explain to the world.

*Explain on, bro.*

Probably best place to start is on my fiftieth birthday, December 16, 2006. This was the winter before your 7/7/7 thing.

*Where were u?*

Sitting in a lonely condo in Las Vegas, Nevada. I had this place at the Metropolis, a supercool ocean-green art deco building on the corner of Desert Inn and Paradise Road. But brother, it was hardly paradise. More hell than heaven—mental hell—cause I was caught between warring feelings. My feelings for Judi and my family and my newfound love for Lorena. Complicating matters was the fact that Lorena was pregnant with our child.

I'd met Lorena on a Southwest flight to New Mexico. She was with her mother. We chatted it up a bit and I invited them to my show. Twenty-one years younger than me, Lorena had all the allure of youth. She was beautiful. She was charming. She was warm. She was intelligent. I could see she was an independent woman. She had cultivated an expertise in cosmetics. She knew makeup better than most seasoned makeup artists. She was strong and she was fun. For the first few months we had a friendship, not a romance. But deep down I knew I was fooling myself. I was involved in a platonic relationship that I did not want to be platonic. When it ceased to be platonic, everything changed. More than being satisfying sexually, it was satisfying spiritually. I loved this woman. I was on cloud nine.

Lorena was seven when she saw *Purple Rain* and, right there and then, decided that Morris was going to be her boyfriend. But I was no longer that playa character. I had stopped playing. I was a grown man with a wife and family. I believed in devotion. I believed in fidelity. Yet I also believed that love can surprise you, even shock you, into doing things you might not otherwise do.

For an agonizingly long period of time I lived in doubt and indecision. Judi knew about my other situation. I didn't have to tell her. She felt it. Women feel those things. I felt that I owed her the truth and confessed. Judi was direct: Did I want to leave her?

At first I didn't think so. I thought I wanted to save my family. Judi would go forward only if we went back into therapy. My attitude about therapy hadn't changed. I still hated it. Maybe because it forced me to face things I didn't want to face.

**Damn right. Judi saw me. She saw MD. And she knew MD was still acting out. MD might not be doing no more drugs . . .**

Not might but *absolutely* not doing drugs.

**But drinking. And liking how booze did what coke had done. Escape. Float above your feelings. Come on, tell the truth and shame the devil. Admit it.**

For years I was straight-ahead sober. Not even wine. Then when I started to have a drink now and then, it was no big deal. I wasn't then, and am not now, a falling-down drunk. Alcohol is something I can take or leave. Never did fuck with my career like coke. I'm cool.

**Says you. But I say the more you drink, you more you wanna drink, and the more you wanna drink, the more you wanna go to something harder, something stronger. You wanna jump back into that rocket ship and zoom to the moon.**

That's where you're wrong. I hear you putting that idea in my head, but it's no longer tempting. I'm too old to fool myself about hard drugs. That rocket ship's gonna have to take off without me.

**But that rocket ship is fueled by more than coke. It's also fueled by ego. Being adored by this fine young woman jacked up your ego and brought me back in your life stronger than ever.**

You want back in my life—that's for sure. You hate it when you can't get control of my head and keep fucking me with your bullshit.

**What you call bullshit I call the motherfuckin' truth.**

The simple truth is that I was torn between two good women. Judi and I had the boys. I hated destroying my family. But Judi's insistence that I do what she say and spend an eternity in therapy wasn't gonna work. That wasn't me. Our lack of sexual sizzle was another negative factor.

Meanwhile, Lorena had moved into an apartment in Bellflower, a suburb southeast of LA. I'd gotten a gig as a cohost on *The Michael Baisden Show*. Michael was a brotha who'd been successful on syndicated radio. Now he was going on TV. We clicked, but not for long. My cohost role was downgraded to musical director. The show, though, never found its feet and there was no longer a reason, other than Lorena, to stay around LA.

So I went back to Atlanta to be with Judi only to return to Bellflower to be with Lorena. I couldn't make up my mind. So on my fiftieth birthday, I decided to be with no one except myself.

That wasn't easy. I put on my old records—those early sides I'd cut with Prince and The Time—and cranked up the volume to where you could hear the funk halfway across Nevada. I heard myself singing "Gigolos Get Lonely Too." I was sure as hell lonely, but was I a gigolo? What is a gigolo? I looked up the meaning in Webster's. It said something about being a promiscuous lover. I didn't see myself as promiscuous, but I sure did sing that song like I was. I turned up the song full blast. I wanted to blast all the indecision from my brain. I wanted to forget the present and live in the past. I wanted to live in the music. I wanted to hide in the music. I wanted the music to tell me what to do. But music is music and life is life, and my life was staring me in the face. I had lived life for fifty years. I had five children. I was about to have a sixth. I had impregnated a beautiful woman while married to a different woman. I was living in a culture that frowned on that. I frowned on that, yet I had caused that. I had every reason to be down on myself. Every reason to crank up the music even louder so I wouldn't have to think, reflect, or decide.

A call came from the building's manager. Tenants were complaining. Turn down the music.

I turned it up.

It's my birthday.

Let them kick me out.

I wanted to be kicked out.

I wanted to cause havoc.

I wanted to act out.

I'd already acted out.

I had two women.

I had to choose one.

I had to turn down the music.

I had to be a respectable man living a respectable life.

I had to do the right thing.

But what was the right thing?

Who was the right woman?

Back to my past family with Judi?

Or go forward with my future family with Lorena?

In the end, the future won over the past.

The decision came after months of going back and forth. I drove everyone crazy. I caused a lot of pain, especially to Judi and our boys.

I did my best to explain, but there's really no way to explain why a man fractures a family. He does it because he does it. He wants something else.

So I turned fifty alone. I turned down the music in my Vegas condo. I got through the night. Two months later Elijah was born. Eventually Morris, Lorena, and Elijah became a family. A second marriage. A new life. A decision that brought joy to some and pain to others. I felt both the joy and the pain.

I moved on only to experience an even greater pain, one I never saw coming.

The decision came after months of going back and forth. I know everyone says it, but I caused a lot of pain, especially to Jodi and our boys. I did my best to explain, but there's really no way to explain why a man fractures a family. He does it because he does it. He wants something else.

So I turned fifty alone. I turned down the music in my Vegas condo. I got through the night. Two months later Elijah was born. Eventually Teresa and Elijah became a family in a second marriage. A new life. A decision that brought joy to some and pain to others. I felt both the joy and the pain.

I moved on only to experience an even greater pain, one I never saw coming.

# 28

# REMEMBRANCE OF THINGS PAST

I would never have read a Shakespeare sonnet if one of my more educated friends hadn't shown it to me. I want to quote it here because it sets the tone I need to tell the rest of my story. The first four lines of Sonnet 30 go like this:

> *When to the sessions of sweet silent thought*
> *I summon up remembrance of things past,*
> *I sigh the lack of many a thing I sought,*
> *And with old woes new wail my dear time's waste.*

Might seem funny that a funkster from Minneapolis would be quoting something written by a British cat over four centuries ago. But the lines hit me hard because I have spent hours silently thinking about what went down back in the day. Like Shakespeare, I regret things I wanted to accomplish but didn't get done. Messing with them devilish drugs, I wasted more time than I wanna remember.

I do remember that my falling-out with Prince happened on 7/7/7 and our reconnection wasn't realized until the winter of 2016. That lapse in our friendship caused pain. But for us to get back together, we had to go through changes.

*Brother, u were always putting me thru changes.*

I was about to say the same thing about you.

*I say it with love.*

So do I. But you can love a person—and God knows, I love you—and still not trust them. After 7/7/7, my trust wasn't there. I could have called you to find out why you threw us off the show. Or you could have called me. But neither of us did. Ain't that some shit? Two cats who came up together. Two cats who jammed together, shared the same humor and sometimes the same ladies. Two cats who deeply understood each other. But you were in your corner and I was in mine.

*Pride.*

Yes, sir, pride will keep you from doing the things that need done. Like reaching out. Like demanding that the dialogue go on. Like jumping on an airplane and just showing up and saying, "Here I am, bro. Let's talk.'

*U could have done that.*

You could have done it too. You could also have told me you were hurting. I had no idea.

*I kept my pain private.*

Or secret.

Life moved on. During the summer of 2008, I was happy that Jimmy Jam and Terry Lewis rejoined The Time for a gig at the Flamingo in Vegas. It was a nice little run 'cause all of us had our own spot on the show. There were the original Time hits like "Cool." I did some of my solos like "Oak Tree." Courtney found a girl who sang like Janet Jackson so Jimmy and Terry could showcase their own brilliant stuff. (It was Jellybean Johnson's groove and production chops, by the way, that helped turn Janet's "Black Cat" into a monster hit.)

Jesse Johnson burned some of his solo singles like "Be a Man," and naturally we put the icing on the cake with "The Bird" and "Jungle Love." When we moved out of the Flamingo, Donnie and Marie moved in. I do believe they're still there.

Meanwhile, Jimmy and Terry, whose love for The Time never died, wanted to cut a Time record. The last one done with the original members was *Pandemonium*, and that was sixteen years before. It was—well, it was time.

When Prince heard the news, he popped up out of nowhere and made it clear the record couldn't carry the name The Time. Turned out after thirty-one years he was reminding everyone that he still owned the name. Yet I'd been touring for decades under Morris Day and The Time, and all that while without a peep from Prince. That was different, Prince's people said. My proper name was in the billing. Because on this new record we wanted to go back to the original name—The Time—Prince wouldn't have it.

Good luck trying to reach him. Good luck trying to have even a two-minute phone call. Jimmy couldn't get through. Neither could Terry. Me either. Prince being Prince was off the grid.

Not wanting to incur the wrath of his Rottweiler lawyers, we said, fuck it. Fuck The Time. We'd call ourselves the Original 7ven 'cause that's who we were—Jimmy, Terry, Jesse, Jellybean, Jerome, Monte, and me. Jimmy and Terry were the prime movers. We cut it in their studio in Santa Monica. It was cool to see old wounds healing before our very eyes. In days gone by, Terry Lewis and Jesse Johnson were like oil and water. But during these smokin' sessions, Terry had a way of calming down Jesse's fiery disposition that made all the difference. All of us together again knew that the Original 7ven was no joke.

"Among the great funk bands," said one reviewer, "this may be the greatest."

We called the record *Condensate*, a word that became a permanent part of my show when, after the release of the record, I began touring again as Morris Day and The Time. I'd open my show with this spoken riff:

"You may notice a bit of moisture on my forehead, a bit of moisture falling about my face. And I know what you may be thinking. You're thinking that maybe Morris has lost it. You may even be thinking that Morris is not cool anymore. Well, let me fix that shit for you. Let me ask you a simple question. When you take a cold bottle of champagne out of the refrigerator and put it on the counter, what does it do? No, it doesn't sweat. It begins to condensate. Condensation happens when you're cool from the inside out. So please understand, Morris is not sweating. Morris is *condensating*. Morris is still cool."

**That was me talking, not you. That was the MD of old, the cat too cool for school. The one who was gonna do whatever he wanted to. The one . . .**

No, sir. Gotta stop you right there. I'm not saying that the blown-up ego voice ever left my head completely. I still hear you from to time. But by this time in my life I knew that the man onstage—MD—was a character who no longer dominated the offstage me. The offstage me—Morris the son, the brother, the father, the husband—had learned the difference between fantasy and reality. Fantasy was thinking that the world owed me. That I was entitled. But reality had taught me that, like the rest of humanity, I had to work. And although Prince was among the great creators of far-out fantasy in the history of entertainment, he was the one who'd schooled me in that work ethic. And it was the work ethic—then and now—that saw me through.

I hate to say this to you, MD, 'cause you're a crafty dude, but your voice, once the loudest thing in my head, is now hardly a whisper.

**So that's it for me? You're banishing me from your book.**

You're in my book. I've given you more space than you deserve.

**I'll be back.**

I'm sure you will. But that don't mean I gotta pay attention. Your job's over. You served a purpose.

**And what's that?**

You showed me that the man I was isn't the man I wanna be. And isn't the man I became.

# 29

# SECRETS

*No one tells all their secrets. Not even u. There's some stuff about u that u r not telling in this so-called tell-all.*

Never said I was telling all. All I said was that I'd try to tell the story as honestly and plainly as I could. And right now, I just plain don't know why you and I let all those years go by with bad feelings still lingering.

*I was the one who reached out.*

I give you the credit. Truly. Because I was stuck on stupid and not about to reach out to you.

*I reached out 2 u. I'd seen u & The Time play the Grammys with Rihanna. Loved seeing that. That's one of the reasons I invited The Time 2 play Paisley.*

And I accepted on one condition. That we got paid. In advance. With a cashier's check.

*Old-school R&B chitlin circuit style.*

You bet.

*Well, I coughed up the money. U got the check.*

And made the gig. The gig was beautiful. Beautiful to see you out front loving what we were doing. Getting down with the crowd. Blowing us kisses. That meant everything to me. 'Cause it's one thing to turn on an audience and give them the pleasure they've been looking for. But, man, it's a whole 'nother thing to see the Founding Father, His Purple Majesty, out there partying like it's 1999.

*It's my band. Y'all are my band.*

More than your band. We're your heart. You gave us your heart. That heart never stopped beating and never will. That night at Paisley we played our heart out. We played for you.

*I felt it.*

After the show I was walking down one of the many hallways at Paisley when I heard someone clapping. I looked behind me and you stepped out of a dark shadow. You were smiling and nodding.

"That was beautiful tonight," you said.

That's when you invited me to hang in that little diner you set up inside Paisley.

*I remember. Judith Hill was there.*

Another great female singer you produced. The album you cut on her, *Back in Time*, was a beauty. Brought back memories of *Musicology*. You had her singing straight-up soul. You had her singing better than ever. She'd been with Michael Jackson. MJ had her duet with him on "I Just Can't Stop Loving You." They were gonna do it on his This Is It Tour, the show that never happened.

Michael's death shocked all of us. I know it shocked you. Whatever the competition between the two titans—and, believe me, the competition was fierce—you saw Michael the same way Michael saw you. You and he had ocean-deep respect for each other's talent.

*& love. I had love for his talent.*

You never failed to recognize talent. What I appreciated about the album you produced on Judith, though, was how you went back to the funky source to plot the funky future. Judith's record was one of the last things you did, and I hear it as one of the best.

So, yes, Judith was there that day at the diner. So were her mom and dad. They were sitting off in a booth. You and I were in another booth by ourselves. You looked great that night. You looked like yourself. You looked happy.

*I was. When The Time throws down, I'm always happy.*

We started talking shit the way we'd always talked shit. Good shit. Deep shit. Back-in-the-day shit. Shit that made me feel that the wounds were healed.

*They were.*

We talked about doing things together in the future. Writing. Recording. Touring.

*We had a plan.*

I could feel you were sincere.

*I was.*

But I didn't know about the pain.

*It was there.*

It didn't show.

*I didn't want it 2 show. What was the point?*

The point is that no one knew. If we'd known, maybe we could have helped.

*Things turn out the way they should.*

I'm not sure.

*I am.*

What makes you so sure?

*I'm just saying that there's divine timing. We met as kids when we were supposed 2 meet. We made the music we were supposed 2 make. We drifted apart when it was time 2 drift apart & came back together at just the right moment. We had the final talk we needed 2 have.*

I'm prolonging that talk in this book.

*I c that, & I've been good enough 2 go along with u. I've lent u my spirit.*

Your spirit haunts me when I think about the last time we were together. I'm haunted by what we said before we hugged and went our separate ways.

"I love you," you said.

"Love you too, brother," I said.

First time those words had been spoken to each other.

*We accepted each other. We accepted love.*

Brother, when I left you in Minneapolis and then, only two months later, heard the news I was a million miles away from acceptance. I was in denial. No, sir, that's a joke. My man is not dead. That's an Internet hoax. My man is not checking out at age fifty-six. Someone's gonna get in hot water for spreading vicious rumors like that. My man takes cares of himself. My man eats health food. Don't even eat no meat. Healthy as a horse. Hates drugs. Drinks a gallon of water a day. Looks twenty years younger than his real age. Playing and singing better than ever. Got another forty, fifty years to live. Got another hundred albums to cut, another thousand songs to write, another ten thousand shows to perform. He'll outlast us all. When it comes to pure energy, he ain't hardly human. When it comes to creative output, he's got no limits. Fuck 1999. He'll be partying like it's 2050.

Word came to me April 21, 2016. My wife, Lorena, and I were on a flight from Vegas to Orlando. Plane landed in Chicago for a layover. Got off the plane and my phone was blowing up. That's when all the denial kicked in strong. Denying everything that I was hearing was true. Then denial turned to prayer. Praying everything I heard wasn't true. Then prayer turned to shock when the truth was confirmed. Then shock turned to grief. Grief stayed, all that day, and the next day and the day after and the week after and the months after that. Grief had me going back to the diner in Paisley Park when I saw you that last time. Our conversation was over. Our plans were set. You're not that much of a hugger, but you hugged me. I'm not that much of a hugger, but I hugged you. You don't usually talk that way but you said, "I love you." I don't usually talk that way but I said, "Love you too, brother."

Did you know? Did you see ahead?

*Can't say what I knew. Can't say what I saw. All I can say is that I've stuck around long enough 4 u 2 tell your story.*

I need you to stick around a little longer.

*Y?*

I can't end it like this. I need another chapter.

*Keep it short.*

I'll try.

# 30

# NOT THE END

Let's do it this way.

*What way?*

Tell the story a different way.

*U've already told it your way.*

Yeah, but I want a happy ending.

*How u gonna manage that?*

Let's start at the beginning. A boy is born in Illinois. His mother moves him and his sister and brother to freezing-cold Minneapolis. They live in the ghetto. The boy falls in love with music. The boy's a natural-born drummer. Practices day and night. Gets real good. Plays along with the hippest fusion and funk records out there. Then one day in a high school lunchroom he hears a band that blows him away. Hears a guitarist who blows him away. Dreams of playing in that band until the dream comes true. The guitarist is also a singer and writer who can dance his ass off. The guitarist is a mysterious cat who doesn't say much to anyone but you can hear the wheels turning in his brilliant mind. The guitarist is shrewd. The guitarist is plotting the future. He and the drummer vibe like brothers. Laugh together. Jam together. Then the guitarist goes off and leaves his band and gets a solo deal in LA.

*U r just telling the same story u have already told.*

Wait. Gonna change it up. The guitarist comes back and gets the drummer. Tells the drummer to be a singer. Tells the drummer to lead a band. Turns out the band is superbad. So now the singer, who used to be the drummer, is even closer to the guitarist. No problems, no jealousy. They go on and make a movie, and then another movie, and then they tour for thirty years without a single argument or fight.

*U r turning it into a fairy tale.*

It could have been that. It should have been that. If I hadn't gone off tripping on drugs, it might have been that. If you hadn't gone off tripping on ego, it might have been that.

*What's the purpose of flipping the script when the script's already written?*

Maybe to show folks how to benefit from how we fucked up. Brothers who wandered off in different directions for stupid reasons.

*But remained brothers.*

And yet couldn't really help each other when help was needed.

*U r into regret.*

I'm just into saying that this story has a message.

*Don't get preachy.*

Look who's talking about getting preachy.

*U haven't let me preach once in this story.*

That's 'cause I don't wanna lose your fans. I want them to know that there's a message to your story and mine.

*So u r gonna turn this into some sentimental cautionary tale.*

Hey, man, ain't nothing wrong with caution. Caution is good. I could have used some caution. I had no pause button. I went for instant gratification. Give me that high. Give me that lady.

I loved and admired your work ethic, but when it came to that shit, you also didn't have no pause button. How many killer shows can you put on before the pace kills you? How much jumping around can you do in those high heels? How much punishment can your body take? How much pain can you put up with before you look for some kind—any kind—of relief? I'm not blaming you. I'm saying . . .

*Saying what?*

Saying that everyone needs balance. And not that I'm saying you're everyone. You're a batshit crazy out-of-your-mind genius at what you do. Genius makes balance that much harder because your brain's moving so fast. But I'm believing even geniuses need balance. Geniuses *especially* need balance.

*I did what I did.*

Yes, and I'm saying I wanted you to do more. I didn't want you to cut out so early. I don't want to be sitting here talking to your spirit. I want to be here talking to you, alive and well and planning your next record.

*B4 u said I worked 2 hard. Now u r saying I needed 2 work more.*

You had more to give. You left before your time.

*Aren't u calling this book* On Time*?*

That's the title.

*Well, maybe I did just that. Maybe I left on time. Maybe there's a divine timing that u don't understand.*

I hear you. And I'm not saying you're wrong. But there are people out there who aren't you and me who can think twice when they read what we did. Maybe they can find their pause button.

*How r u defining the pause button?*

I guess I'm calling it God.

*Wow. I wasn't expecting that.*

I wasn't either. It just came out.

*U better explain.*

No big explanations. God is love, and love wants us to slow down and make sure we ain't hurting nobody, including ourselves.

*That's it?*

You told me to keep the chapter short.

*So u don't need me anymore?*

I'll always need you

*& I'll always b around.*

# 31

# THE BEGINNING

At age sixty-two, I like looking at the big picture—past, present, and future. Like always, my picture is completely musical. It's the musical picture that has always kept my overactive mind in focus.

At the start, the focus was funk, and funk remains the solid bottom line. I'm believing that, like the blues, funk will always be a living presence. Maybe that's because like all the great forms—jazz and gospel, for instance—funk is based on the blues. And the blues, as we know, is the human condition. If we're alive, we struggle. The blues tells the story of that struggle, just as my funk reveals everything I've gone through. The beautiful part is that in singing the blues, you lose the blues; in playing funk, you break out of your own funk. You're relieved, released, and set free. Thank God for musical expression.

As a kid, funk hit me first. Credit James Brown. But he wasn't the only godfather. Other musical forces, like Sly and the Family Stone and Tower of Power, also swept me up. Fusion spun me around, making me realize how much harder I had to work to attain the musical proficiency of artists like Tony Williams and Billy Cobham. Groups like Return to Forever and Weather Report washed over me like a tidal wave. Rather than drown, I learned to swim. I learned from the bebop giants like Art Blakey and John Coltrane's brilliant drummer Elvin Jones.

I saw Rick James bridge the gap from George Clinton to Prince, who, of course, became as great as any master before or since. But during these heady days and nights when our funk was being formed, another musical stream began to flow. *Prince,* his second album, was released in 1979, the same year that the Sugarhill Gang's "Rapper's Delight" exploded. Folks forget that 1982, the year of MJ's *Thriller,* was also the year of Grandmaster Flash and the Furious Five's "Message." The birth of hip-hop was as important as the birth of the blues because again, like soul and jazz, it was based on the blues. It was based on inner-city struggle.

All the giants to follow—Kurtis Blow, LL Cool J, NWA, Ice-T, Public Enemy, Snoop, Nas, Tupac, Biggie, Jay-Z, all the way to Drake, Kendrick Lamar, J. Cole, and Travis Scott—are heavyweights. On a different path, they created a deep and serious art form that resonated the world over. Once again, black music created a new avant-garde. I watched it all unfold.

So last year when word came down that Snoop Dogg was looking to hook up with me, I was a happy man. I've long looked at Snoop as one of the baddest street poets.

He invited me down to his elaborate recording complex near LAX. First thing he said, in his inimitable molasses-thick kickback flow, was "Man, I've always considered myself an unofficial member of The Time. If the Original 7ven has an eighth man, that's me."

Turned out Snoop's a soul scholar. In addition to his rap chops, he knows him some gospel, R&B, and funk. He knows The Time catalog better than I do.

When he gave me the tour of his studio, he stopped before a mural he had commissioned illustrating all his idols. Among those depicted—Marvin Gaye, Curtis Mayfield, Michael Jackson, Prince—was me. I was surprised and humbled.

"You on the wall, dude," he said. "Now I got you in my studio. And I got a track you gonna love. Feel like singing?"

How could I say no? He'd invited a whole lot of people to hear me, so naturally I agreed. In truth, it isn't my style to try out new material in the studio with a crowd standing 'round. Especially strangers. But since Snoop was treating me like royalty, and since I did love the track he'd laid down, I went into the booth and sang my heart out.

Guess I did okay because next thing he got 1500 or Nothin'—a killer production team—to start writing for me and got Moe Z, another unheralded genius, to supervise what turned out to be one of my funkiest records.

So I stop where I began. Loving on music and its power to reinvent.

To refresh. To revitalize. To surprise.

Music that comes from the past, keeps me in the present, yet pushes me into the future.

The musical future is bright because the funk ain't lost none of its strength. Funk ain't going nowhere.

Might have a different flavor, but funk's funkier than ever.

Funk's forever.

And with that, let the church say . . .

***AMEN.***

# ACKNOWLEDGMENTS

Writing this book has been both therapeutic and more rewarding for me than I ever could have imagined. None of this could have been possible without the loving support of my beautiful wife, Lorena Day. Thank you for being my rock, my strength, and my peace.

I'm forever grateful for my loving mother who gave birth to cool (me). She showered me with unconditional love, was the first to cultivate my talents, and, through all the ups and the downs in my life, forever remained in my corner.

To my children: Tionna, Taj, Evan, Derran, Cameron, and Elijah; grandchildren: Asiah and Naomi; and my great-grandchild: Noah. No matter what I've accomplished in my life, you're all my greatest gifts.

To my brother and tour manager, Jesse. I couldn't imagine doing all of this without you, bro. It feels good knowing my blood has my back, no matter what. Thank you for all that you do. Love ya, man.

To my manager, Courtney Benson. Whenever my phone rings and I see it's you calling, I know you've got another idea to keep the Morris Day show rolling. I appreciate your commitment to cool, my brotha. Keep shining, C-Biz.

A very special thank-you to my brilliant band—especially my day ones, Jelly Bean Johnson and Monte Moir. We go back like rocking chairs. My main man Ricky Freeze Smith, Tori "Freak Juice" Ruffin,

Thomas Austin, and Jeffery McNeely. Thank you for sticking with me and keeping "The Time" legacy alive. Love you guys.

Shout out to the rest of the original "The Time" members. Jimmy "Jam" Harris, Terry Lewis, Jesse Johnson, and Jerome Benton. Love you fellas! Couldn't have done it without you.

My book publishing family—David Ritz, thank you for your brilliance and commitment to this book, and to my editor Ben Schafer and his team, thanks for working so hard to get this book done.

Thank you to all and any that have been part of this journey with me, and instrumental in my career. There are too many to mention by name, but if you know me and I know you, this thank you is heartfelt. And an extra-special thanks to all my fans around the world. Love you all.

Last but not least—my brotha from anotha mother, Prince. Thank you for your vision, for challenging me, and for being the master of what you do. Man, I wish I could pick up the phone and just call you and see how you're doing. Miss you a great deal. Just know, I'm keeping the funk alive for ya. Still puttin' that "chili sauce" on 'em . . . WaHa!!!!

CPSIA information can be obtained
at www.ICGtesting.com
Printed in the USA
LVHW101532070222
709842LV00010B/133/J

9 780306 922213

31901067715724